Learning objectives, task setting and differentiation

Learning objectives, task setting and differentiation

Trevor Kerry
College of Teachers
International Institute for Educational Leadership
University of Lincoln

First published in 2002 by:
Nelson Thornes Ltd
Delta Place
27 Bath Road
CHELTENHAM
GL53 7TH
United Kingdom

02 03 04 05 06 / 10 9 8 7 6 5 4 3 2 1

A catalogue record for this book is available from the British Library

ISBN 0 7487 6858 0

Page make-up by Acorn Bookwork

Printed and bound in Croatia by Zrinski

CONTENTS

FOREWORD

The material in this book was published previously under the same title but this volume has been subject to a number of significant revisions and updates. The book is prefaced by a new editorial and a revised section on how to use the manual. All the material has been linked specifically with the National Standards for qualified teacher status, and there are connections made to other government reports and papers (see Key references section on page xii). New material, for example on the subject of homework, has been added. While the text and Activities remain mainly unchanged, each chapter is preceded and concluded with a panel to guide the reader's learning. Dated material has been excised. The intention is that, in its new format, the material – all of which has been composed and trialled in real classrooms or with teachers under-going professional development – will help Key Stage 2 and 3 teachers along with students in training for these age-groups to gain immediate access to these crucial skills.

EDITORIAL

The world of education, and above all of educational organisations, changes at an ever-increasing pace, but the need for teaching skills remains a constant in this sea of change. Of course, the skills themselves have to be reassessed, updated, amended and refined. This is the purpose of the present series of books: to take a practical but analytical look at teaching pupils at Key Stages 2 and 3.

The series brings together experts in the field of pedagogy, covering key issues in the art and science of teaching. It is interesting to reflect that, after 150 years of compulsory education for all children, this country still does not have any posts in colleges or universities that are overtly about teaching skills, i.e. pedagogy. There are lecturers in subject areas, professors in education, and education management gurus – but not a single professor of pedagogy. That fact alone must indicate the value that books like this have in helping practitioners in a far too neglected field.

The series is deliberately cross-phase in its approach. There are two reasons for this. The first is that the fundamental skills required of the teacher at these two levels are essentially the same or similar. The second reason is that the latest government thinking, encapsulated in its 2001 White Paper, highlights both the transition from primary to secondary schools and what it sees as the relatively poor performance of Key Stage 3 teachers. Indeed, the Government implies that it would like to see approaches at Key Stage 3 become more like those at Key Stage 2. However, while governments define policy, it is left to practitioners to work out those policies in practice, as here.

But this series also has a context in those very educational changes that we have mentioned. The teaching profession, at every level, is still coming to terms with two decades of far-reaching innovation. These are just a few of the, universally significant, events that have happened in that time:

- The establishment of governing bodies with extensive powers and legal responsibilities
- The introduction of a National Curriculum along with several major emendations of it and its operation
- The requirement for teachers to undertake professional training and development on a minimum number of days per year
- The reform of educational finances and the growth of cheque-book schools
- The demise of Local Educational Authority powers in many areas of operation
- The institution of Ofsted inspections
- Requirements for appraisal of teachers
- The compulsion for assessment of pupils through SATs
- The insistence of the Government that schools publish their league tables of results

- The introduction of literacy and numeracy hours in primary schools – a move towards increased prescription over what is taught, and how it is taught
- Compulsory processes for the monitoring of the performance of head teachers
- The positive and financially tangible encouragement of the adoption of ICT as a fundamental way of working in schools
- Innovative routes into teaching such as the SCITT schemes
- The rise in the use, and variety of use, of support staff in schools
- Encouragement of the establishment of schemes of private–public partnership in school funding
- New standards published by the Teacher Training Agency for the training of teachers.

The list could be extended, but the reader will already have grasped the enormity of change on the professional life of teachers. The list doesn't deal with the more intangible changes that permeate the education environment: changes to philosophy, theory and approach. These include things as varied, and as wide-ranging, as: the growth of concern in educational psychology with multiple intelligences; the imposition of political philosophies such as marketing schools; the invention of management practices such as reengineering; the growth of practical proposals such as changing the school calendar from three to five or six terms; or conditions of service issues such as the introduction of performance-related pay. What an exciting and varied life we in the teaching profession lead!

In this ocean of innovation, teaching skills remain an island of calm on which all who provide services to pupils in classrooms must retain their hold and on which they must focus. Teaching skills are not a refuge from change: indeed they change with the shifting situation. But they are root skills that teachers need. In this series we look at some of those key skills, reinterpreting them for today's classrooms and learning situations, and recognising the continuing and important role they play in realising the potential of students and pupils. The series covers such essential topics as managing the classroom efficiently, formulating learning objectives, asking effective questions, explaining clearly, setting worthwhile tasks to pupils, and using ICT to best advantage and with confidence. Our intention is a simple one: more effective teaching.

Trevor Kerry, series editor
2002

ACKNOWLEDGEMENTS

Material for Chapter 8 (The purpose of differentiation) and Chapter 9 (Differentiation in practice: the teachers' perspectives) has been taken, in part, from an article previously published in *Educational Studies*, volume 23, number 3, 1997. The author would like to thank the Editor of Educational Studies, Carfax Publishing, and the co-author of the article, Carolle Kerry, for permission to use this material.

How to use this book

This teaching skills series of books is designed to fulfil two closely related but not identical intentions for teachers in training, newly qualified teachers, and others who want to examine their practice more closely. The first is to help you become a 'thinking teacher', and the second is to encourage reflective practice.

The literature of continuing professional development for teachers and managers is full of references to reflective practice. The point of this approach is that the professional – in whatever role – is able to stand aside from himself or herself and to take an objective look at their own behaviour and actions as well as those of others. From this objective approach he or she can learn – can reflect upon practice – and can mould behaviour to be more productive.

To be a 'thinking teacher' is slightly different. It implies that you have a curious mind: one that questions, is open to ideas and change, that investigates problems rather than accepts the solutions of others, and that sustains a degree of intellectualism in all that you do. This approach is, after all, what you are trying to encourage in your pupils. This is something that is highlighted in Hay McBer's (2000) Report as one of the professional characteristics, or what it calls 'deep-seated patterns of behaviour'.

To achieve these ends, the books in the series are closely modelled on the requirements for teachers as drawn together in two crucial pieces of official literature: the Hay McBer Report (2000) already mentioned: a Report commissioned by the Government to draw together aspects of good practice in teaching; and the Teacher Training Agency's (TTA) National Standards for Qualified Teacher Status.

Within the books, each chapter is constructed so as to:

- Indicate the learning about the specific teaching skill that is outlined in the chapter
- Provide suitable text, with illustrations and examples, to carry the reader through the learning process
- Include useful checklists, Tables and Figures to break up the text and to serve as *aides-mémoire*
- Invite participation in learning through Activities designed to improve your skills
- Summarise the key learning points at the end of each chapter.

It is important to stress that the material is all real. By that is meant that every classroom example has been used in, and culled from, an actual classroom where the activity reported was used successfully. There are no fictional examples. Furthermore, the material in the chapters has all been put to use in national training courses that have run successfully and been repeated several times: every Activity may not be equally practical or feasible in every school, but all the Activities have been used by teachers and they are tried and tested material that has received professional approval.

It is also imperative to point out that teaching skills, and the thinking that underpins them, are not free from controversy or debate. Indeed, part of the professionalism referred to by Hay McBer is to engage in precisely those debates. Thus the reader must not assume when reading the books in this series that he or she will not be challenged to engage in that debate at times: it would be a mistake if this were not the case. Nevertheless, the authors of this series, experts in their fields, have not peppered its pages with academic references; these last are used sparingly so as not to interrupt the flow of the text.

This, and the other books in the series, are designed to take the reader on from knowledge to skill in an interactive way, through using the Activities and through trying out ideas in the practitioner's own classroom. Some people will find the learning process easier if they maintain a reflective log, however brief, or use a tape recorder to play back parts of their lessons for later analysis, or work with a colleague who can observe them and give feedback (team working is favoured by both Hay McBer and the National Standards documents).

In practice the books can each be used in a variety of ways:

- As a continuous text: the reader then just reads over the Activities as they arise
- As a training manual: in which the reader pauses at the Activities and tries them out
- As a source book: the reader can dip into specific sections for particular help and guidance.

Similarly, the context in which the texts can be used will vary. In many instances, a book will simply be read as a text for self-development by a teacher working alone. In other cases, a school may adopt the title as part of its in-house training programme, and colleagues will discuss and share its text and Activities as on-going professional development. There will be some who use the text as part of training conferences or lectures. The material should prove invaluable to teachers in training and as a support for teaching practice. The outline of skills in each title may also be adapted by heads, and others who act as appraisers, as a guide to their observation of, and feedback to, colleagues.

These are books about what happens 'at the sharp end' – in the classroom.

KEY REFERENCES

Department for Education and Skills (2001) *Schools achieving success.* London: DfES

Department for Education and Skills (2002) *Education and Skills: Delivering Results – a strategy to 2006.* London: DfES

Hay McBer (2000) *Research into Teacher Effectiveness.* Report by Hay McBer to the Department for Education and Employment, June 2000

Teacher Training Agency (2001) *Standards for the Award of Qualified Teacher Status.* London: TTA

Teacher Training Agency (2002) *Qualifying to Teach.* London: TTA

Note

TTA (2001) was produced as a consultation document. It contained two sections – the National Standards (statutory) and the Handbook (non-statutory guidance). Following the consultation period there was considerable objection to the Handbook element as being too prescriptive. The decision was made, we understand, by TTA to rewrite this latter element. At the time of compiling this book only the statutory Standards had been revised – TTA (2002), also referred to in the text as QTT. This was a fairly superficial document lacking as it was a version of the Handbook from TTA (2001). For this reason, and because we believed that the original Handbook gave important clues to the way that government thinking was working – which might operate during inspections, for example – we have chosen to retain reference to this document as the Draft Handbook. The updated version of the Handbook, promised for Spring 2002 by TTA, was still not available in June as this text went to press.

OBJECTIVES

This chapter invites you:

- To consider what learning objectives are and their definition
- To divide learning objectives into five domains
- To see how learning objectives in the five domains build into the objectives for a lesson/scheme
- To put learning objectives into the context of pupils' needs, abilities, experience and opportunities.

TOWARDS A DEFINITION

Learning objectives are hedged around with unnecessary mystique. They are, quite simply, the answers to this question:

At the end of this lesson/session/term/year, what do I want my students to know, to do or to understand which will take their learning on from where it is now?

It is probably worth pausing over this definition.

Many readers will recall the laboured hours spent preparing for teaching practice, during which time you were required to write lesson notes. The most difficult section was always the bit which asked you to identify your aims and objectives for the lesson. Indeed, most people have great problems in sorting out the differences between these two items. For my own part I have a simple rule-of-thumb for distinguishing between them.

Aims: are long-term, all-embracing and tend towards the philosophical or ideal. For example, in a technology lesson on cooking, a long-term aim might be to encourage students to work safely in the kitchen (keeping hair away from flames, guarding hands from the oven with appropriate protection and so on). Every lesson would aim to teach safety (or hygiene, or high standards of presentation, etc.) or to reinforce it.

Objectives: are shorter-term, immediate and rapidly testable. So, in the cookery lesson, the immediate objective is to make an edible steak and kidney pie. This may involve learning some new skills of food preparation, or an understanding of how to make particular kinds of pastry. But the end-product is judged by its edibility, taste, look, etc.

Other writers talk about learning objectives using other kinds of description. For example, in the National Standards for Teachers (TTA

2001) the formulation of learning objectives is explicit in the section on planning teaching. For qualified teacher status, practitioners must have high expectations of pupils based on evidence of their past and current achievement, the standards expected of the relevant age group, and the range and content of work expected of that age range. These expectations must be used to set clear teaching objectives and to translate these objectives into learning targets that are explicit for pupils. Such targets have to be formulated in the light of the context in which classes at Key Stages 2 and 3 operate in respect to such constants and variables as the need to include learning through ICT, to encourage cross-cultural learning, and to make use of out-of-school learning contexts such as museums and field work or, at Key Stage 3, employment-based settings. These same aspirations are echoed in QTT paras 2.2–2.5, and especially in section 3.1 where all the same key ideas recur.

Despite these definitions, though, there is a simpler way to think about what lessons are hoping to achieve. This is to use the word **intention.**

Intention is a generic term which can cover both the aim of a lesson or series of lessons, and the objective. Intentions can be shorter-term or long-term. The long-term intentions of our cookery classes are to encourage safety in working, hygienic practice and high standards of presentation in food preparation. The short-term intentions are to enable the students to create specific dishes, or to make particular items such as types of pastry.

Although this is a chapter about learning objectives, the little word intention will be a most useful one to have in mind to help cut through the jargon. It will, perhaps, help with the next point, which is that learning objectives are often divided into what are called **domains.** There are five domains which feature in this classification, but for the moment we shall look in detail at just three:

- the knowledge domain
- the skills domain
- the domain of understanding.

We must now look at each of these in turn to see what exactly each means in the context of a lesson.

Learning objectives in the knowledge domain

These answer the question:

> *At the end of this piece of work/session, what do I want the students to know that they did not know before?*

Teachers spend a lot of their time in class talking: the intention of much of that talk – at least in part – is that students should know some new material at the end of this process. Part of the purpose of schooling is to impart knowledge. Indeed quite a lot of the curriculum is predicated on the assumption that, having worked their way through the syllabus of a subject or a topic, students will know certain things as a result. These things are often tested in examinations and assessments, and are typically subject to periodic feedback by teachers on progress through classroom tests.

While it could be argued that too much emphasis is placed on students acquiring factual knowledge (i.e. pieces of information – as opposed to the understanding of the implications of that information), one cannot deny that a significant intention of schooling is to teach specific pieces of knowledge: how to read; the basic number bonds; the history of Britain; what certain words mean in a modern language; the format for writing a letter; the names of the notes in a musical scale; what the scale on a map is for – and so on. Every lesson implies intentions – i.e. learning objectives – in the knowledge domain. To identify those key elements of knowledge is, in effect, to formulate the learning objectives for the lesson.

Let us take a very simple lesson. The topic is Adaptation, which comes from the Life and Living Things element of the National Curriculum in science. Our imaginary teacher begins from a visual aid: a stuffed owl. Having settled on the topic, and having acquired her visual stimulus, she now has to begin to formulate the learning objectives for the lesson. In the knowledge domain, what is she intending to achieve? Since the concept of adaptation implies knowledge of the lifestyle (the cluster of phenomena to which it has adapted), she must be intending that the students should know about the owl's lifestyle: i.e. where and how it lives. This is the new knowledge which will flow from the lesson: so to impart this knowledge in some way must form part of the knowledge objectives of the lesson.

Our teacher may formulate a learning objective for the lesson thus:

At the end of the lesson (I intend that) the students will have learned some aspects of the owl's lifestyle.

The National Standards (as set out in TTA 2001 and subsequently in QTT – TTA 2000: see especially section 2) are strong on knowledge, because they are predicated on the National Curriculum. They required qualified teachers to teach the 'required or expected' knowledge relevant to the curriculum for the age range for which they are trained – in our case at Key Stage 2 or Key Stage 3. The Draft Handbook exemplifies content work across various subject areas, in English – for example – talking about planning, organising and teaching coherent English lessons that set teaching and learning targets and plan for progression against age-related expectations and assessment information. Key Stage 2 teachers are required to teach across the curriculum. For Key Stage 3 teachers, in QTT para 2.1c we read:

For Key Stage 3, they (teachers) know and understand the relevant National Curriculum programme(s) of study, and for those qualifying to teach one or more of the core subject, the relevant frameworks, methods, and expectations set out in the National Strategy for Key Stage 3. All those qualifying to teach at Key Stage 3 know and understand the cross-curricular expectations of the National Curriculum and are familiar with the guidance set out in the National Strategy for Key Stage 3.

But knowledge, in itself, is not the whole story of a lesson's experience for the students. So what else forms part of the learning intentions?

Learning objectives in the skills domain

Learning objectives in the skills domain require an answer to the question:

At the end of this lesson/session, what do I want my students to be able to do that they could not do before?

It might be thought, at first glance, that lessons in some subjects are more overtly skills-based than others: that design and technology lessons are more skills-related than English lessons. But that analysis will not stand scrutiny. It is fairly easy to catalogue skills across the curriculum – all of them implicit in the National Curriculum for various Key Stages. For example:

- In a geography lesson – to be able to create a map of a given area (be it the school playground or a selected piece of the outdoors);
- In a music lesson – to be able to tune an instrument;
- In a history lesson – to be able to use an index to locate information about a specific historical character;
- In an English lesson – to be able to punctuate one's own work accurately using not only full stops and commas, but also semicolons and speech marks;
- In mathematics – to be able to look up log tables;
- In art – to be able to mix a colour to the shade required;
- In drama – to be able to control the voice to speak louder and softer, but still be heard by the audience;
- In IT – to know how to use the Edit facility;
- In science – to be able to handle acids safely.

All of these processes depend to an extent on the student's knowledge, but that knowledge has to be applied to some form of action. Students have now taken some responsibility for translating their knowledge into performance. Most lessons have skills elements embedded in them. In identifying the learning objectives of lessons, teachers need to recognise what these elements are and to formulate them appropriately in learning objectives.

So let us return to the hypothetical lesson our imaginary teacher was giving about Adaptation. She has it in mind that the students need to look hard at the stuffed owl in order to begin to work out how it lives (that it has a hooked bill for tearing flesh, for example). Observation is important in science and is a skill. She will want them to draw the owl in order to record their observations. Later – when they have learned more about the owl's digestive system, which is specially designed to cope with bone and feather – she will want the students to dissect pellets of these materials regurgitated by the owl in order to identify items in the owl's diet. The observation, the drawing and the dissection all require skills.

So the teacher might formulate some further lesson objectives:

At the end of this lesson (I intend that) the students will have observed accurately and acutely the main features of the bird.

At the end of this lesson (I intend that) the students will be able to use their observation skills to draw a reasonable representation of the bird, showing its main features.

At the end of the lesson (I intend that) the students will be able to dissect an owl's pellet efficiently.

So now the students will have both a knowledge of owls which will lead them towards the concept of Adaptation, and the skills to carry out scientific work more effectively. However, they will still be lacking an important feature of classroom learning.

Learning objectives in the domain of understanding

Learning objectives in the domain of understanding answer the question:

What do I want my students to understand at the end of the lesson which they did not understand before?

Knowledge without understanding is a sterile accomplishment. Long John's parrot may have been able to trot out information overheard from drunken sailors, but it would have done him no good because he didn't know how to put the information to use! In a companion volume in this series time was spent on looking at how explanations 'give understanding to another'. In our imaginary lesson on Adaptation, the teacher wants the students not only to acquire some facts about owls and their lifestyle, but to manipulate those facts into an appreciation of how the owl – over time – has evolved to deal with its lifestyle:

- Its head – can swivel in a wide arc in order to see prey without having to move and create noise.
- Its feet – are covered in hair to deaden the sound of its take-off prior to pouncing.
- Its talons – have evolved into stiletto sharpness for killing and holding prey.
- Its wings – have specially adapted feathers which make its flight silent.

From these observations, the link between the observed characteristics of the owl and the knowledge about its lifestyle gradually builds into a picture – a conceptual map – of the relationship between form and behaviour. This conceptual map we call **understanding**.

Real learning consists of acquiring, making sense of, relating and synthesising many such conceptual maps. Moving learning on requires the teacher to build new concepts effectively and to give students the opportunity to test them and make those links.

So the teacher in our hypothetical lesson may formulate some further learning objectives, this time in the domain of understanding:

> *At the end of this lesson (I intend that) the students will be able to understand how observed features of the owl's anatomy have evolved to assist its lifestyle.*

> *At the end of this lesson (I intend that) the students will have acquired a conceptual grasp of the key technical term 'Adaptation' with a view to linking it to other technical language ('evolution', an idea already introduced to the class; and others, such as habitat, to be introduced later).*

The National Standards (TTA 2001) demand that teachers can identify the knowledge, skills and understanding to be covered in lessons, 'with appropriate reference to Programmes of Study, QCA frameworks and other non-statutory guidance as appropriate'. QTT (TTA 2002: Introduction) asks that teachers 'be confident and authoritative in the subjects they teach in relation to knowledge and understanding. In looking at the first three learning objectives we have covered those requirements, but the time has come to take stock of those three objectives and how they work together in a lesson.

Taking stock of learning objectives

This is an opportune moment to pause and take stock. In trying to illustrate how learning objectives work, we have hypothesised a lesson on Adaptation, starting from a stuffed owl, and led by a teacher who has formulated three kinds of learning objective: of knowledge, of skill and of understanding. So, if this teacher were writing down those objectives (let us say as part of the set of lesson notes which she has to produce for a visit by an Ofsted inspector), what would she put? This is what she has collected so far:

> *At the end of the lesson (I intend that) the students will have learned some aspects of the owl's lifestyle.*

> *At the end of this lesson (I intend that) the students will have observed accurately and acutely the main features of the bird.*

> *At the end of this lesson (I intend that) the students will be able to use their observation skills to draw a reasonable representation of the bird showing its main features.*

> *At the end of the lesson (I intend that) the students will be able to dissect an owl's pellet efficiently.*

> *At the end of this lesson (I intend that) the students will be able to understand how observed features of the owl's anatomy have evolved to assist its lifestyle.*

At the end of this lesson (I intend that) the students will have acquired a conceptual grasp of the key technical term 'adaptation' with a view to linking it to other technical language ('evolution', an idea already introduced to the class; and others, such as habitat, to be introduced later).

This list is quite impressive, and gives a good flavour of the kind of intellectual learning which will be taking place in the lesson. The Ofsted inspector will be in no doubt, on reading the notes, what the teacher's intentions for the lesson are. Both the inspector and the teacher, in their different ways, will be able to gauge student progress against the objectives – a point to which we shall return later in the book. But the form of the objectives listed above is a bit clumsy and long-winded – many teachers would feel threatened about having to produce so much paper for one set of lesson objectives. It has been convenient for us to record them in this way in order to identify the thought processes which underpin them. Now we can begin to shorten the format. What our imaginary teacher might write could be something nearer to this:

LEARNING OBJECTIVES FOR THE LESSON:

Students will be able ...

- to learn some aspects of the owl's lifestyle;
- to observe accurately and acutely the main features of the bird;
- to use their observation skills to draw a reasonable representation of the bird showing its main features;
- to dissect an owl's pellet efficiently;
- to understand how observed features of the owl's anatomy have evolved to assist its lifestyle;
- to acquire a conceptual grasp of the key technical term 'adaptation' with a view to linking it to other technical language.

Our imaginary teacher has done quite a good job so far of generating learning objectives which are meaningful (that is, they give students real and measurable targets to achieve); which are based on sound theory (for example, they move from the concrete through the conceptual to the abstract); and which are simple to understand (so that an observer can track what is happening). Before you proceed any further in this chapter, perhaps it is time to take stock, too, of your own approach to composing learning objectives by undertaking Activity 1.

Activity 1

Exploring your own learning objectives

Find some recent lesson notes which you have made. Go through them, and pull out the learning objectives you have composed. Do they fall into the three domains described in this chapter:

- knowledge
- skills
- understanding?

Are any of these domains under- or over-represented in your learning objectives?

Do any of your learning objectives appear to fall outside these three domains? In what ways?

(Keep a notebook of your responses to each Activity in this book as you come to it. This will build into a learning resource.)

THE INTER-RELATIONSHIPS BETWEEN LEARNING OBJECTIVES

However, you may have discovered through Activity 1 that not all learning objectives are quite as easily categorised as those which have been used as examples so far in this chapter. This is because – in formulating an objective – one often needs to mix elements from two or more of the three kinds discussed so far: knowledge, skill and understanding-related objectives. An example may help.

As the work on Adaptation unfolds, our imaginary teacher is intending to use information gleaned from the dissection of pellets. The dissection will reveal what the owl has eaten during the last few hours: probably some combination of rodents (rats, mice, voles) and various beetles. By gathering a lot of data from the class's dissection of pellets it will be possible to get some feel for the proportion of different foods eaten. This the teacher wants the students to display in the form of a pie-chart. Her learning objective is:

To turn data gained from a study of pellets into a pie-chart.

Such an objective requires a mix of abilities from the students. They must have a knowledge of how to construct pie-charts; and an understanding of how the data is to be acquired and displayed. If they use a computer to generate the chart they may need key-boarding and IT skills. This learning objective, then, crosses the domains previously identified; and the teacher needs to be aware of this.

Further domains for learning objectives – 1: the attitudinal domain

Not all learning objectives have to relate to the actual knowledge, skills and understanding that students acquire. It is equally legitimate to formulate learning objectives about the **way** in which such learning is acquired. One of the concomitants of the learning gained is the attitude to learning which students receive through their experiences of school. Think back for a moment over your own education: what did you hate most? For many it was mathematics; and what we learned in maths was often to dislike maths more! But what if the opposite had happened?

In recent years successive political administrations have made much play of the need for teachers to teach subjects and to 'communicate a love of the subject' to their students. While it is certainly possible to argue a case that subjects are less (or at least no more) significant than the interrelations between them, it remains true that the distinctive elements of subjects – what are often referred to as the 'disciplines' of the subject – can be a source of fascination. To pick up on this fascination is precisely the point of learning objectives in the attitudinal domain.

Hay McBer (2000) calls this attitudinal domain 'a passion for helping pupils to learn'. The Report identifies five levels of activity that illustrate and exemplify this teaching skill:

- Creating a learning environment – e.g. by making the classroom an attractive, comfortable and stimulating place
- Showing how – e.g. by clear explanation and demonstration
- Supporting practice – e.g. by engaging pupils through use of questions
- Driving for understanding – e.g. making pupils work things out for themselves
- Motivating pupils to learn independently – e.g. by providing opportunities to show that self-learning is enjoyable.

Such objectives could be written for the Adaptation lesson. They might include:

By the end of the lesson (I intend that) the students will have understood some of the mystery surrounding owls and their life-style ...

or

By the end of the lesson (I intend that) the students will have discovered the fun of engaging in scientific enquiry through exploring a real problem (i.e. the dissecting of pellets exercise).

However, the attitudinal domain is not the only other domain worthy of mention here.

Further domains for learning objectives – 2: the affective domain

Not only is the way in which students learn important, but the **context** in which that learning takes place may also be significant. Explicit reference to the affective domain is rare in both Hay McBer (2000) and the TTA (2001, 2002) because both tend to concentrate on the teacher, and the teacher's relation to the learner, rather than the learners' relations with each other. However, the importance of this aspect of classrooms is implicit in both sources. In a companion book in this series there is a review of some of the most influential learning theories currently recognised as useful. Among these theories is Social Constructivism. Constructivism itself suggests that students learn through the interaction of thought and experience; Social Constructivism emphasises the part played by others in that process. Social

9

Constructivists understand that the social relations, communications and conversations between teacher and student and between student and student, all help to promote the learning that takes place. Social Constructivism highlights the role of classroom organisation for learning in enabling students to communicate freely: for example, through group work or discussion. The principles can once again be applied to the formulation of learning objectives. Thus our imaginary teacher of Adaptation might have included in her learning objectives one in the affective domain:

By the end of this lesson (I intend that) the students will have promoted their learning through working collaboratively in groups to dissect their pellets and collect data from the exercise.

Collecting the learning objectives from the five domains

So we are now in a position to draw together all the learning objectives formulated in this chapter – those from the first three (cognitive) domains, and those from the latter two (process) domains. The result looks like this:

LEARNING OBJECTIVES FOR THE LESSON:

Students will be able ...

- to learn some aspects of the owl's lifestyle;
- to observe accurately and acutely the main features of the bird;
- to use their observation skills to draw a reasonable representation of the bird showing its main features;
- to dissect an owl's pellet efficiently;
- to understand how observed features of the owl's anatomy have evolved to assist its lifestyle;
- to acquire a conceptual grasp of the key technical term 'Adaptation' with a view to linking it to other technical language;
- to understand some of the mystery surrounding owls and their lifestyle;
- to discover the fun of engaging in scientific enquiry through exploring a real problem (i.e. the dissecting of pellets exercise);
- to work collaboratively in groups to dissect pellets and collect data from the exercise.

This set of objectives is quite impressive, emanating as it does from a lesson, or short sequence, on the theme of Adaptation. What has emerged from the formulation of them is, hopefully, the understanding that these intentions are not bolt-ons to the lesson, but entirely integral to it. The irritation which many teachers express when faced with having to generate learning objectives can be overcome through practice, because the formulation of objectives should be part of a teacher's daily professionalism. What many practising teachers and teachers in training have to learn, is how to think in intentions: to develop the mind-set that stands back from the teaching process and can analyse it objectively in this way. As professionals we are accountable, and that means being able to answer questions such as:

- Why are you teaching this material?
- Why are you teaching it like this?
- What are you hoping your students will achieve as a result?

Learning objectives serve this purpose for us in our daily lives.

LEARNING OBJECTIVES: PULLING TOGETHER THE THREADS

Having established what learning objectives are, and to some extent how they can be arrived at, it is time to deal with a few other insights into the learning objective process.

This chapter has suggested quite forcefully that all learning objectives have two essential components:

- **An intention on the part of the teacher;**
- **A learning outcome to be gained by the student.**

So, in composing learning objectives, teachers have simply to ask themselves the two key questions: what do I intend this lesson/session to achieve, and what will the students gain from it? The gains are then defined under the five domains described above (and see also Figure 1.1).

These five domains will become the subject of the next sections of the book, and their significance will be drawn out and the inter-relationships between them explored.

One difficulty which teachers tell me they have in drawing up learning objectives relates to what might be called 'the chicken and the egg' question. That is, which comes first: the lesson or the objective? In

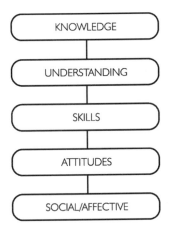

Figure 1.1

Learning objectives: the 5 domains

Figure 1.2

Some factors in composing learning
objectives

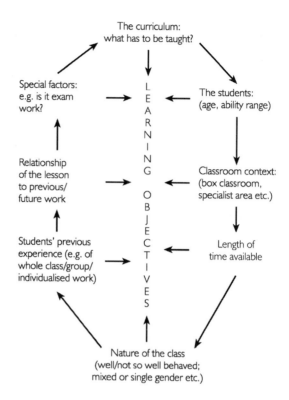

other words, should I devise my lesson and then write the objectives? Or do I write some objectives and then fit the lesson round them? The answer is much the same as the one in the chicken-and-egg conundrum! Perhaps Figure 1.2 will help to throw some light on the fairly subtle inter-play between these components.

Figure 1.2 emphasises that the curriculum is more than the knowledge base that is prescribed by, for example, the National Curriculum or a school document. Students come with different levels of knowledge and begin from different starting points of understanding. The physical surroundings of the teaching space will determine what is taught and how. The amount of time available will also condition the depth of exploration that is possible; and there is a fundamental need to establish good relations in the class for lessons to be successful anyway. Teaching modes (whole class, group work or individualised learning) also affect what can be taught and to whom. The nature of the work (for examinations or for some other immediate purpose) and its place in a sequence of lessons will determine how the teacher approaches it and what learning objectives are appropriate. All these issues will be exemplified as the book progresses.

The last task for you in this chapter is to review some of your own practice in establishing learning objectives in your teaching situation by tackling Activity 2.

Activity 2 ———————————————————

Improving your own learning objectives

Look back to the learning objectives you used in Activity 1 – these were drawn from some recent lessons which you had taught.

Now try to improve on the objectives you wrote at the time, using the insights gained from this chapter.

You may add objectives to those you originally composed.

Assess the improved insights this process has given you into your own teaching.

Outcomes

At the end of this chapter you should have:

- Understood the definition of learning objectives and the five domains
- Taken account of contextual issues and the learning environment in formulating learning objectives
- Practised formulating learning objectives, and reflected on this process.

LEARNING OBJECTIVES: SOME UNDERLYING ISSUES

OBJECTIVES

This chapter invites you:

- To reflect on short, medium and long-term planning
- To consider the factors that influence the identification of learning objectives
- To consider the social contexts in which learning objectives operate
- To look at the classroom planning cycle
- To recognise your own bias in formulating learning objectives.

THE NATURE OF THE PROBLEM

As I was writing this chapter I came across a very persuasive short paper by an American named O.L. Davis Jr. Davis's argument is simply this: that curriculum and teaching are intentional; they influence but do not cause learning. In recent years, especially in Britain, politicians have espoused the belief that if curriculum could be improved, then standards would rise. The result of this enterprise was the National Curriculum. Few teachers seriously believe that students necessarily perform better as a result of it, yet that was its intention. Since its intention did not seem to work particularly well, the politicians sought others: they invented schemes for 'improving' teaching, such as the 'Advanced Skills' concept, and for holding up high performing or 'Beacon' schools as exemplars. Again, intentions, but as yet still proving themselves in the scheme of things. And so Davis concludes that much of this enterprise is futile; and in a poignant passage he describes the failure in a metaphor:

> *Remember the British experience in the trenches that snaked across northern France in the Great War. For four years, the pride of England formed in ranks, charged across no-man's land, and were mown down like grain at harvest time ... Unfortunately, the end of the story is known. The German trenches held ... British valour did not cause victory simply because generals ordered or desired victory.*
>
> (Davis, O.L., Jr (1998) 'Curriculum and Teaching: no guarantees of learning'
> *Education Today*, vol. 48.2, pp. 28–31)

Curriculum and teaching, Davis goes on, are not consequential but intentional; they intend but cannot guarantee learning. So is learning a hopeless case? No, for Davis maintains:

teachers must teach more mindfully in order that their actions begin to match their principled and rich intentions.

(op.cit. p. 31)

This book began by formulating learning objectives as a precursor to students' learning. Just as the British generals needed not more charges but better tactics to succeed, so for teachers – in order to translate intentions into learning – they need better skills and strategies, of which the formulation of effective learning objectives is just the beginning. As the book unfolds the relationship between learning objectives (teaching intentions) and learning outcomes will be explored. For the moment, however, let us pause over some of the ways in which learning objectives can be turned into tactics for improving learning.

The long, the medium, and the short

In practice the learning objectives which teachers formulate tend to relate to one of three time-scales:

- **long term** – things that need to be achieved through the syllabus/curriculum for the year
- **medium term** – things that need to be achieved this term
- **short term** – things that have to be achieved this week or in this lesson now.

The Draft Handbook (TTA 2001) points to the fact that planning has to be carried out in different time contexts. Teachers must be able to 'use teaching objectives to plan lessons, and sequences of lessons', and to 'plan sequences of lessons to ensure progression in the short, medium and longer term, as appropriate to the school's own curriculum planning documentation'. The same sentiments appear in QTT para 3.1.2.

This time-scale issue is quite important. The longer-term goals tend to drive the shorter-term ones. However, longer-term goals tend to be more general: more akin to what we called, in the previous chapter, aims. By contrast, the short-term goals are more akin to what we labelled objectives. Long-, medium- and short-term goals are all valuable in giving both direction and purpose to learning: to setting out the intentions. Perhaps some examples of long-, medium- and short-term learning objectives will illustrate this.

Examples

In English, a long-term learning objective might be to encourage students to compose poetry of their own to a reasonable standard using both creative thought and an adventurous approach to form and style.

The medium-term objective for term 1 could be to expose the students to some exciting poetry: simply to capture their interest in the form, the narratives, the rhythms and the language of poetry. In term 2 the teacher might move on to the narrower learning objective of understanding how rhythms are made up through the closer, more technical examination of different types of poem: the haiku, the limerick, the epic form, and so on. By term 3 the learning objective might have shifted to students writing their own compositions based on one or more of these models.

The short-term learning objectives would relate to individual lessons. One such lesson – picked at random from a series – might be guided by the objectives that, at the end, students will be able to:

- read and enjoy the 'Smuggler's Song';
- understand the narrative;
- appreciate the rhythm;
- explain the purpose of the refrain;
- appreciate that the refrain changes connotation from verse to verse, e.g. from humorous to sinister;
- make a start on preparing a narrative and rhythm of their own, prior to attempting to write to the model.

The learning objectives, regardless of time-scale, do not simply happen. All sorts of factors influence the objectives which teachers formulate; and it is to some of these factors that we now move on in the next section of the chapter.

FACTORS INFLUENCING LEARNING OBJECTIVES

In the previous chapter it was suggested that a number of factors played a part in helping to determine learning objectives. These were:

- The curriculum: what has to be taught?
- The students: age, ability range.
- Special factors: e.g. is it exam work?
- Classroom context: box classroom, specialist area etc.
- Relationship of the lesson to previous/future work.
- Length of time available.
- Students' previous experience (e.g. of whole class/group/ individualised work).

These are all factors which are quite closely related to the immediate circumstances of the school, the school day and the classroom. But there are other factors – more theoretical factors or factors external to the teacher – which also influence the learning objectives teachers set.

The first group of these additional factors relates to *how* learning takes place. In formulating learning objectives teachers take into account the teaching methods which will best achieve those objectives. For example, it is hard to teach debating skills with students seated in rows listening to a lecture about them! Similarly, we hear a lot about the need for students to develop effective self-study skills; yet this is hardly achievable as an objective unless students are given tasks which allow them freedom to think for themselves. It fails if they are subjected to too much supervision. Students can't develop creative thought if what they produce has to be honed all the time to a teacher's very personal and narrow view of what constitutes excellent work. This last point may need some illustration.

Imagine a primary classroom in which students are studying the Second World War. The teacher has collected some posters of the time, and found a tape of contemporary sounds such as sirens, fire engines and the noise of bombing. The children listen and discuss these in a whole-class setting. Then they are set to work. But not only is the task identical for each child, even its parameters are highly circumscribed. They are to produce a story of a night in the Blitz under a given title. They must write between 15 and 20 lines. Their work must contain reference to each of the sounds they have heard. They are given a character around whom to hang the event. The story must contain the words: Spitfire, London and shelter. They must indicate how Londoners suffered. They are not given access to additional materials. There is to be no conferring. The end-product is to be illustrated with a picture of a plane, and the main colours are to be red and black.

Far-fetched, do you think? Not really. A bit caricatured, perhaps, and from time to time there is a case for delimiting tasks like this. But too often both the spoken and non-verbal approval which teachers signal for classroom thinking (or lack of it) stifles creativity in otherwise quite dynamic minds.

Another influence on what kinds of learning objectives are formulated relates to the ways in which students are grouped for learning. Narrow streaming of students may influence what happens in class towards a static, desk-bound approach based substantially on listening to the teacher, followed by all students attempting an identical task. By contrast, individualising work may enable a student with a specific flair to do a task beyond the range of others in the group, yet cater simultaneously for the youngster who needs a simpler activity aided by a classroom assistant. Whole-class work, group work – for example for role plays – and individualised work all have a place in learning. Matching desired outcome (the learning objective) to the appropriate grouping method will produce more effective learning besides improving the variety of lessons and thus sustaining student interest more effectively.

The Draft Handbook makes it clear that teachers must take proper account of pupils' individual needs and backgrounds. They must plan 'for the varying needs and achievements (of pupils) as appropriate to gender, ethnicity and social background' and they must 'clearly outline suggested teaching strategies and suggested grouping arrangements'. The requirements, with minor semantic changes, are recycled in QTT section 3.

The third of this cluster of issues relates to matching teaching and learning styles in the classroom. Teacher A may teach more effectively through exposition and didactic methods; teacher B may be a skilled exponent of group work. Each will tend to formulate objectives in ways which can be achieved through these methodologies. But, equally significant, students may have preferred learning styles. One may really enjoy working alone, while another may long for the anonymity of whole-class activity. The crucial consideration here is balance; and therefore setting learning objectives such that they demand this balance from a week's, a term's or a year's work, is an important part of planning for teaching.

Hay McBer asserts that 'effective teachers employ a variety of teaching strategies and techniques to engage pupils and keep them on task. Despite this assertion Hay McBer goes on to emphasise teaching rather than learning, or the match between the two. This is because, in practice, learning strategies are rarer to spot in classrooms than teaching strategies. However, Hay McBer did note that:

> *individual work and small group activities were regularly employed as ways of reinforcing pupil learning through practice and reflection. However, it was evident that when effective teachers were not actively leading instructions they were always on the move, monitoring pupils' focus and understanding of materials. Content and presentation were varied to suit the needs of the class and nature of learning objectives.*

Activity 3

Considering a range of teaching methods

Part of the skill of the successful teacher is to vary his/her teaching methods in order to achieve the learning objectives for the lesson by using appropriate teaching methods. The following is a list of some teaching methods. Think back over your last term's teaching. How often did you use each method? Add any other categories you wish to list:

Teaching method used:	often	occasionally	never
Exposition			
Questioning			
Practical work/experiments			
Problem-solving			
Simulation			
Role play			
Practice tests			
Debate			
Team teaching			
Self-study by students			
Written exercises			
Peer critique			

Self-marking by students			
Others			

Now scrutinise the results of this exercise. How varied is your teaching? If it falls into predictable patterns, can you suggest reasons why?

A second cluster of factors which influences the kinds of learning objectives that are set relates to the group of people whom we might call clients of the education system. These include, for example:

- Ofsted
- Parents
- Governors
- Politicians.

TTA (2001) deals in only a cursory way with these issues. There is a requirement for the qualified teacher to 'communicate sensitively and effectively with parents and carers' (para 1.4). There is a brief mention of 'planning collaboratively for the deployment of additional adult support' (in other words managing, or helping to manage, support staff), a theme picked up also in para 3.4.9 where teachers have to be 'open to being observed teaching'. However, this area of professional life is under-represented in the document. The theme is picked up equally briefly in QTT para 1.4.

We need to look at each group of clients to try to assess its influence on learning objectives.

Ofsted inspectors work to a closely delineated set of criteria for judging the effectiveness of schools. They need to be assured that all the statutory criteria for education are met, that policies and other paperwork are in place, and that school governors are overseeing the delivery of curriculum in the school. They measure students' progress and attainment, and they assess the teaching, and the response from students to that teaching. Though the official line might be that no one philosophy of education or style of delivery is favoured by Ofsted, many teachers will be suspicious of this. Many teachers respond to this covert pressure by shifting their lessons and planning in this direction, at least when an inspection is likely or imminent.

Parents can have a strong influence on teachers' planning, and hence on their learning objectives. Parents of primary students may want to see evidence of 'hearing students read', or of the 'testing of tables'. They may be quite hostile to legitimate educational activities, the value of which they do not understand but which can be labelled 'play' or 'topic work' or whatever they have been conditioned to believe is the bogey of the educational system at that moment. Similarly, parents of students moving towards GCSE/GCE examinations will, naturally, be concerned about results and may blame the methods of teaching if the results do not match their own expectations.

School governors play a similar role in a different forum. Since, in the post-Thatcherite market economy (which remains unreversed under New Labour), schools now have to compete for students and recruit against the threat of closure, governors want to see results too. Again, teachers may feel constrained to limit their teaching methods and cram students for examinations or assessments simply to satisfy their governing bodies.

Much of this pressure itself comes, ultimately, from politicians. One could argue that it is a bad thing when politicians take no interest in education: the financial and other provision tends to lessen. One could argue, too, that it is a worse thing when they do take an interest: they tend to set up agendas which are more political and less educational! The stress of this situation was well summarised recently by Karen Thornton in an article in the *Times Educational Supplement*:

> *A curious mixture of pragmatism and idealism characterises the work of the Government group charged with finding, disseminating and implementing good teaching practice. Pragmatism, because the members want to produce practical and effective guidance for schools. Idealism, because they see the key to the whole process in the more esoteric area of tapping teachers' own creativity, boosting professional confidence and status, and encouraging reflective practice. The tensions thrown up by these two approaches ... look set to keep the nine-strong team busy for some time to come.*
>
> ('In search of excellence', *TES*, 15.5.98, p. 20)

The simple truth is that one can't have a reflective profession, learning from its own action-based research and development, when there is strong external pressure from the political masters of the system to follow a specific dogma and adopt 'preferred' procedures.

So one set of factors influencing the formulation of learning objectives relates to educational issues such as the use of appropriate teaching methods, intelligent grouping strategies, and varied teaching/learning styles. Another set of factors is that relating to satisfying the various and varied 'clients' of the education system. A third set of factors relates to the 'customers' of the system: the students.

Students themselves have views about how their education should proceed: perhaps the older the students the more articulate they can become about expressing these views. However, even young children can reflect on their own learning and how they learn best: what is known as metacognition. The very best teachers try to get their students to articulate how **they** think they learn effectively, and will use this data in formulating their learning objectives for lessons.

It is surprising how little of the documents TTA 2001, 2002 or Hay McBer's Report deals with pupils as opposed to teachers. Hay McBer talks at length about classroom climate, but little about students having a direct input to their own learning and preferred learning methods, though there is current debate about pupils assessing teachers.

You can see from the argument of this section of the book that formulating learning objectives is not an easy task, nor is it one to which no preconceptions are brought. In the Editorial it was suggested that this volume, like others in the series, aims to equip teachers with skills suitable for the twenty-first century. Such schools will be increasingly subject to the kinds of external pressures described here: and the skill of unmasking those pressures and dealing with them professionally will become increasingly important.

So what has this chapter told us so far about learning objectives and their formulation? Perhaps we could summarise it thus:

- Learning objectives are 'intentional' – they don't guarantee learning will take place.
- There are many educational and non-educational pressures which operate on teachers when they try to set learning objectives.
- Nevertheless, learning objectives are important: without intentions there can be no planned consequences.
- The nature of the intentions (or learning objectives) has a significant influence on the consequences: i.e. whether learning takes place effectively.

So how are the consequences to be realised?

EFFECTIVE PLANNING

Formulating lesson plans is part of the larger planning process through which all teachers must go in order to teach effectively. Ofsted inspectors still claim that too few lessons are planned effectively. Yet planning is not such a difficult process. Many effective planners use a proforma of some kind to guide their thoughts. Figure 2.1 offers one such proforma – not as an exemplar, but simply as an aid for anyone without a preferred system. The advantage of the proforma in Figure 2.1 is that it helps the teacher to articulate carefully the learning objectives for the lesson.

The traditional classroom planning cycle looks like that in Figure 2.2, and many teachers will be familiar with this. However, for the present purpose an additional dimension has been added: the place of learning objectives (LOs) as central to what happens in the cycle. Learning objectives feed into and out of the cycle at every step. They inform the planning and preparation stage of a lesson. Hopefully, when the lesson is presented, the learning objectives will be implemented. Whether they have been or not will become clear at the assessment stage (whether that is informal assessment through teacher questions and feedback, or whether it is more formal measuring of learning through testing of some kind). Then the results of the assessment will feed into and inform the planning stage for the next lesson, will alter how material is presented, and so on.

COMING TO TERMS WITH PERSONAL BIAS

This chapter has been about the influences that can operate on the formulation of learning objectives. We have looked at this topic as a

Figure 2.1

Lesson planning proforma

Date: **Class:**

Subject:

Lesson objectives (knowledge, skills, understanding, attitudinal, affective)
At the end of this session the students will be able to:

1

2

3

4

5

Outlines of content and sequence

Relationship with other learning

Materials and resources

Teaching and learning methods

Tasks to be set/methods of differentiation

Student assessment

Lesson evaluation

---

precursor to translating effective learning objectives, through good preparation, into effective learning. Yet there is still one further influence which has to be revealed and recognised: the personal bias of the teacher.

The kinds of learning objectives you set will depend upon a number of very personal issues, among the most important of which are:

- your view of curriculum theory

Figure 2.2

Teachers must not lose track of the planning cycle

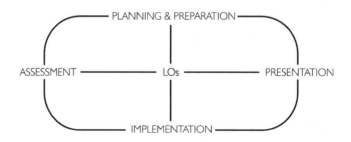

- your philosophy of education
- your preferred teaching style.

The last item has been touched on already in this chapter; so here we shall concentrate on the first two items listed. The argument runs like this:

- Your biases will subconsciously determine the nature of the learning objectives you set and ways in which you try to achieve them.
- Recognising your personal bias will help to free you from too closed a view of your intentions for your students' learning.
- Therefore, finding a way to explore your biases is important.

In this book, the way chosen to explore bias is to ask you to complete Activity 4.

Activity 4.

Recognising your personal biases

Below this Activity you will find a series of statements. Be honest, and cover all except the first one. Now read this first statement, and try to assess the extent to which you agree with it, or why you disagree.

Once you have had this 'internal debate' with yourself, uncover statement 2, and do the same thing again.

Repeat the process one statement at a time.

Assess your own biases towards the educational process based on this exercise. How do they condition your teaching behaviour?

Taken in isolation, each individual statement here would be acceptable to many teachers: how tolerant would you be of those holding each of these views?

At the end of this exercise you should have articulated to yourself something of your beliefs and values in relation to your professional role as a teacher.

Statements relating to Activity 4: exploring bias

Education	is a good thing
Education	should include moral learning
Education	is best located in schools
Education	is ultimately a vocational activity
Education	in Britain should be dominated by a Christian ethos
Education	is incomplete without an introduction to politics
Education	opens minds to change
Education	opens doors to discontentment.

NB There is no 'correct' answer to Activity 4.

Outcomes

In this chapter you should have:

- Thought about the issue of formulating learning objectives over time
- Considered the wide range of teaching methods available to you, and how these can help in formulating effective learning objectives
- Understood some of the external pressures and influences on the formulation of learning objectives
- Recognised some of your personal bias as part of your reflective approach.

LEARNING OBJECTIVES IN PRACTICE

OBJECTIVES

This chapter invites you to:

- Engage with the concept of intellectual climate
- Explore the relationship between learning objectives and learning outcomes
- Consider assessment and recording
- Make use of metacognition as a learning tool
- Recognise the link between learning objectives and target setting

SOME PREREQUISITES

Let us take stock for a moment of what we have suggested so far about learning objectives. They are the intentions for learning which teachers have for students at the end of a lesson, session or longer period of work. They can be influenced by a range of in-school and external factors. In themselves, they form no guarantee that the learning outcomes will be achieved; but, through more general lesson planning, they are a step on the road to achieving these desired outcomes. In this chapter we begin to look at how they can be operationalised.

In practice, there are three preconditions which are required before good learning objectives can be formulated, and before the teacher's intentions for learning can be achieved. One could argue that, in schools for the future, these three items have to become the watchwords of good professional practice. They are:

- a climate of psychological security;
- a climate which values intellect;
- a climate which encourages debate.

Let us examine each of these propositions in turn.

The first thing to say is that learning objectives – poorly constructed – can be purely mechanistic. They can consist of items such as the following.

Students will be able to:

- recite the rules for ...
- list the dates of ...
- recall the story about ... and so on.

So let me declare a bias here (refer back to Activity 4). We have established in Chapter 1 that learning is not on a par with what Long John's parrot could do. It involves processes beyond the mindless stimulus-response of trotting out 'correct' answers. It demands that students **think.** However, thinking is a dangerous process. For one thing, one can think 'wrong' answers. An important part of thinking is speculation, and this may lead to the 'step in the dark' which may prove to be incorrect. How will the teacher react to this? Sadly, there does appear to be a view of teaching and learning which suggests that *learning right answers* is more important than thinking out – despite a few false starts – *really insightful answers* for oneself. Such a view has missed something vital.

Regurgitation is a low-level exercise: the real skill is to break new ground. But breaking new ground may meet a hostile response from a teacher anxious about getting on and getting things 'implanted' in students' minds, especially in a climate of assessment. For a student to be willing to engage in a genuinely cognitive process he or she has to feel totally secure that the teacher will react positively, even to well-thought-out errors. That is what is meant here by psychological security.

The second point – that intellect has to be valued – relates quite closely to the first. Thinking things out – cerebration, to use a technical term – is rarely high on society's agenda of desirable characteristics.

Today's icons are hardly the intellectual elite! Sing a song with pointless words, kick a round collection of leather panels into a piece of net strung between two bits of wood, or sit in front of a goldfish bowl making ambiguous and pointless predictions in a silly voice about winners in a game of chance and you can rise to fame and fortune. Invent something to improve all our lives and no one will ever hear your name. That is the agenda of society. So it can be no wonder to us that those of our students with enquiring minds try to hide the fact – too often for fear of reprisals out of class; nor that the majority of the male student population thinks that 'it's naff to be a boff'. Teachers have to rescue society from this abyss: no one else will. But real learning can take place only in a climate which acknowledges intellect, which accepts and celebrates it and its achievements. The ethos of the school and of your own classroom is critical.

The third point is that learning objectives can be achieved only in a climate which encourages debate. This is the natural outcome of the first two. Intellect has to be traded in order to grow. Students have to be free to express their cerebration; they have to engage in debate not only with other students but with the teacher: and to do it on equal terms – that is, to know that they may sometimes lose the argument and sometimes win it. We're not, of course, talking here about questioning the teacher's authority or the school rules. We are dealing with the intellectual content of the material being taught; and – surprise though it may be to some of the population – there may be fewer 'right' answers than one is sometimes led to believe. Indeed, one could go as far as to suggest that an over-conviction of rightness stands behind most conflict in the world. This is not to suggest there are no absolute or universally desirable values; only that many conflicting groups claim to have exclusive use of them! Dogma has to be replaced by intellect wherever it occurs (and however strongly one would like to agree with it!).

Activity 5

Coming to terms with your own classroom climate

Tape-record one of your own lessons.

Later, play over the tape and try to assess the extent to which you create an appropriate climate for effective learning.

Use the criteria described in the chapter as a guide:

- Do you create an atmosphere of psychological security?
- Do you signal that you value intellectual activity?
- Do you encourage debate (teacher–student; student–student)?
- What could you do to improve your performance on these criteria? Establish a plan for working on any weaknesses which this exercise has revealed.

You may feel that this section of the book has proved to be a controversial one on many levels. Perhaps the argument can be summed up like this:

- To achieve real learning outcomes in classrooms, there can be no ambiguity about whether students are required to speculate.
- To this end teachers need to question students rigorously – and students must not find this intellectual challenge threatening.
- Students' contributions have to be valued – not only by the teacher but by other students.
- Teachers have a duty to recognise that student achievements in knowledge, skills and understanding must go beyond formal assessments (SATs, GCSEs) and not be limited by them.

Classroom climate is given a central place in the thinking outlined in the Hay McBer Report. There it is defined as: 'the collective perceptions by pupils of what it feels like to be a pupil in any particular teacher's classroom, where those perceptions influence every student's motivation to learn and perform to the best of his or her ability' (para 1.4.1). Classroom climate depends not on one teaching skill, but many (some of which are dealt with in companion volumes in this series), e.g. class management. In fact, Hay McBer's research (para 1.4.4 onwards) suggests that three key factors intermingle to make up this climate: lack of disruptive behaviour, encouragement of pupils to engage in learning, and consistently high expectations of the pupils by the teacher. The Report maintains there is a correlation between these three 'latent variables' and student performance. This text would not disagree with the broad principles outlined in Hay McBer, if only because this insight is hardly new, and would come as a surprise to few experienced teachers.

If you would like to get inside the skin of empathy a bit, you might care to try the next Activity – Activity 6. Some time ago I was asked to deliver some in-service training at a school that had had an adverse Ofsted report. I agreed to do this, but only on condition that I spent a day at the school first, attempting to explore the school ethos for myself, since it – above all – was the target of Ofsted criticism. The result was that I came to some clear and simple conclusions about why Ofsted had come to its judgement: lessons were noisy, even committed pupils were distracted, and good lessons went unheeded through poor class control. At the beginning of the in-service day I asked staff to undertake Activity 6. They did it honestly, and revealed that they were well aware of the real problem.

However, it is important to give a word of warning. Reduced to a few simple statements in a Report or a Standards document, the issue of climate looks obvious. In practice it is the outcome of a range of factors (beyond the scope of this book), many of them very subtle, and the interplay between them. So bear climate in mind as a prerequisite of good learning, but do not conclude that that defining it is easy or that a few mechanistic techniques will produce it.

Activity 6

An empathy game

This is an empathy game – but a game with a serious intent.

Imagine you are a pupil in your own school. Below are seven aspects of how you might feel about the school. Each is measured on a 5-point scale (5 = high). Read each item and quickly decide which level of feeling (5 always – 1 never) would apply to you.

Item	Always	Often	Sometimes	Rarely	Never
Motivated	5	4	3	2	1
Threatened	5	4	3	2	1
Making progress	5	4	3	2	1
Interested	5	4	3	2	1
Excited about school	5	4	3	2	1
Able to concentrate	5	4	3	2	1
Valued as a person	5	4	3	2	1

Study your responses and assess what the pattern of scores tells you about the climate in your own institution.

TURNING LEARNING OBJECTIVES INTO CRITERIA FOR LEARNING OUTCOMES

In the previous section it was suggested that for learning objectives to be achieved there needed to be a climate of learning which was characterised by the value placed on intellect or thinking. Within this climate students will learn effectively. To track whether the learning objectives, formulated using the five domains and the various teaching skills articulated in Chapter 1, are being achieved the scene has to shift from simply planning lessons to their implementation. In order to do this we can look at some approaches to 'planning plus implementation' based on the work of real teachers. The first example is of medium-term planning (i.e. weekly planning in this case) by a primary teacher and looks at learning objectives mainly from the teacher's perspective.

Figure 3.1 shows the teacher's planning sheet for the week, which includes her main learning objectives.

Figure 3.2 is the teacher's own assessment of where she believes the students have reached at the end of the week.

In practice these two Figures are two sides of one A4 sheet which the teacher uses to track her own (and the students') progress. Side one (Figure 3.1) records her intentions, side two (Figure 3.2) her assessment of the outcomes. Over time, this kind of recording builds into quite a significant dossier of student learning outcomes.

Of course, each individual lesson (or related sequence of lessons) is planned too. Each lesson plan has its individual learning objectives. Figure 3.3 shows a lesson plan for a lesson on Weather for a mixed group of students in Key Stage 2. The plan follows the format of the kind described in Chapter 2, and it includes the teacher's evaluation of the extent to which the learning objectives were achieved.

The examples show how learning objectives can be built into lesson planning, but how they can then be used to guide the delivery and implementation of the lesson and, finally, to assess the achievement of the lesson. In this way the intentions are translated into outcomes.

Part of the Draft Handbook documentation (TTA 2001, e.g. para 3.1.3) insists that teachers should be able to 'use teaching objectives and learning targets to plan lessons, and sequences of lessons in a way which shows how pupils' learning will be assessed, taking account of and supporting the varying needs of pupils'. Assessment features strongly in QTT, where it is stressed that teachers must make use of a range of strategies for assessment towards planned learning objectives. They must give immediate feedback (i.e. within lessons), and must be able to relate pupils' progress more generally to such criteria as Early Learning Goals, National Curriculum stages and objectives from the national strategies. Able pupils and those with learning or other difficulties should be adequately supported. Progress must be recorded and proper use made of records to report on progress to relevant others such as parents (TTA 2002 paras 3.2.1–3.2.7).

Figure 3.1

Teacher's Planning Sheet

Weekly planning: activities, aims, organisation w/c 14.4 Mon. Training day – mathematics; Wed. – governors' meeting; Thurs. field trip to Lincoln; Fri. – contact SEN service re Tracey	
English	On-going: handwriting, spelling, quiet reading Writing: to help the students record events effectively 'The most interesting event of the Easter holiday' Reading: (older, better readers) to sustain concentration
Maths	Gp 1: Rounding to nearest 10; estimating – worksheet 41 To work in pairs quietly and compare results Gp 2: Calculator work based on Nelson scheme To carry out simple operations accurately; to check by other means Gp 3: Money maths page 43; extension sheets for more able To work accurately setting out examples correctly All: mental arithmetic – To increase speed/confidence
Science	Continue tadpole diary To observe closely and draw accurately
History/ Geog.	Visit to Lincoln (from this very rural environment) To be prepared for the urban scene To be able to record observations using check-sheet
Art/Music	Visit to Usher Art gallery, Lincoln, as part of field trip To sketch cathedral using examples in gallery as a source of ideas about style Composing a piece to create the atmosphere of the city To decide on appropriate instruments and the kind of sounds one would want to use to make 'city music'
RE	Use the visit to the cathedral to think about calmness To encourage students to articulate the idea of calmness through discussion during the cathedral visit
DT/IT	Continue work on their 'concept cars' To solve construction problems as they arise
PE	In PE – passing and catching balls, various sizes, types To improve co-ordination In swimming – revision of crawl stroke To improve confidence and skill

Figure 3.2

Teacher's Evaluation Sheet

w/c 14.4	**Weekly evaluation**
English	Change of plans within school timetable, so handwriting transferred to next week. Reading, very quiet, purposeful The recording task – focused on a single event – did produce some quality writing. Curt made particular progress by using good detail and excellent description. Some effective discussion came from this activity – creative ideas from Sam, Jason and Tammy
Maths	Numeracy/mental work for all: an increasing confidence, though some (esp. Greg) still rather slow Gp 1: Curt, Tracey struggled with estimating, most others secure in the concept Gp 2: Enjoyment in calculator work high. Understanding good overall. They understand the need to check. Jane said: You need to check because you might press a wrong button without noticing and get a silly answer Gp 3: Better as an activity perhaps, using the Shop Tessa understands but is struggling to set sums out tidily enough, so gets confused
Science	A lot of awe and wonder in observing the pond Excellent detail in drawings so we made a collage of them
History/ Geog.	Students well prepared for urban landscape, but the traffic tally proved difficult – they are insecure in a noisy situation – will try this activity in a different location Use of check-sheet to record buildings seen was done well by everyone, so we have some data to take back to school
Art/Music	Drawing the cathedral captured their interest; various styles chosen. Tern, Gail and Nick produced outstanding views City music was popular – Jason a bit silly with the drums! However, Will put together really good rhythms for assembly
RE	Sense of awe readily described by the students
DT/IT	Students made their own links between 'concept cars' and the City visit – Ben modified his design to take up less space in the crowded streets, and we were all able to discuss this
PE	Catching is improving for most except Julie; Jason has excellent co-ordination. Swimming cancelled: bus failed to arrive – objectives transferred to next session

Subject:	**Maths – the weather Y5, 6**
	NC area – handling data
Date:	**17.5–19.5**

INTENTIONS (Concepts, skills, understanding, attitudes, affective domain)
At the end of the lessons students will be able to:
1   Understand that weather varies across the country/world
2   Use maths to study weather phenomena/data
3   Understand and read block graphs with confidence
4   Solve simple problems using skills learned, in sequence
5   Enjoy the experience and relate positively to it
6   Work alone with confidence

OUTLINE OF CONTENT & SEQUENCE
Slides and photographs: Fenland, Lake District, Fuerteventura
Discuss differences; draw out possible reasons for these
Introduction to block graphs, with examples
Use specially prepared weather booklet to practise skills and set problems

RELATIONSHIP TO OTHER LEARNING
Links with geography topic work places
Students have been collecting their own weather data from instruments in school grounds
Links to previous work in maths on 'mean' and 'modal'

MATERIALS AND RESOURCES
Special booklet
photos and slides
slide projector; also whiteboard and pens

TEACHING AND LEARNING METHODS
Observation – Group work
Questioning – whole class
Didactic – (explanation: use of block graphs)
Individual work – use of workbook

TASKS/DIFFERENTIATION
Use of workbook
Differentiation by outcome: examples are graded so most able will get further

STUDENT ASSESSMENT
To show facility with block graphs; to understand how to retrieve data and express it

LESSON EVALUATION
Lesson sequence enjoyed by all pupils
Most understood the block graph – one or two struggled: Angela, Dick
Many more than I guessed went onto the most complicated examples: esp. Terri, James, Dawn, Hannah. Rod and Denise found the early work too easy.
For some, computational skills let them down though concept understood (Terri, Dawn)
One mum told me her son had demanded that the family visit Fuerteventura.

LEARNING OBJECTIVES IN THE ASSESSMENT OF TEACHING

Earlier it was noted that one of the areas upon which Ofsted inspectors comment, and concentrate, is teaching. In the current system, teachers are graded and their grades fed back to them as part of the follow-up to inspection. It is legitimate to ask, therefore, how learning objectives are viewed by Ofsted. The answer is more cryptic than the question. The source of evidence has to be the Framework for Inspection documents for primary and secondary schools (1995); and these yield few direct clues. My reading of them, however, suggests the following.

Ofsted expects that 'there should be clear evidence of programmes of study in the classroom work observed'. So teachers, in their lesson notes, need to articulate those links. The Framework documents also indicate that inspectors expect that 'students are able to cover the required material in appropriate depth'. This statement is content-led and begs a number of the cognitive questions of the kind discussed in the previous chapter.

An important criterion for Ofsted is whether there is 'continuity and progression'. The argument here is that, if learning objectives are clearly formulated, and if they can be seen to be translated into learning, there is clear evidence of continuity and progression for the students.

Ofsted looks for a 'whole school' approach with 'learning outcomes monitored by senior staff' – a statement which suggests that (though valuable when adopted by individual teachers) the learning objective approach suggested in this book would be valuable for whole schools to adopt as part of their teaching and learning policy.

On knowledge, understanding and skills, there is within Ofsted the expectation that 'teaching methods and organisational strategies are employed to achieve stated goals'. One would argue here that the stated goals certainly include learning objectives for the short, medium and longer terms; and that this statement supports the view expressed in Chapter 2: that teaching methods and matters related to grouping and teaching style dealt with earlier (see pages 17–20) are indeed assessed during inspection.

Ofsted also looks for:

- careful assessment based on regular observations;
- whether formal records are to be kept;
- equality of access and opportunity.

Each of these items is or can be dealt with, in part at least, through setting appropriate learning objectives; and the material in Figures 3.1, 3.2 and 3.3 illustrates acceptable ways of documenting that these things are happening consistently (i.e. whether there is an inspection going on in the school or not).

Finally, Ofsted states that 'what is taught' is more significant that 'what is documented'. Most teachers would be sceptical of this declaration. On a lesson by lesson basis, inspectors **do** look for documented evidence of what is taught and criticise any lack in this area. The teacher who leaves to chance whether an individual inspector can deduce the learning objectives of a lesson without documentation is playing Russian roulette!

So, while the guidance is small and often unclear, there are enough clues here to say that the formulating of learning objectives, combined with evidence of their delivery and the monitoring of their success, will be a valuable asset in an inspection.

QTT is actually quite explicit compared with previous documentation. In para 3.2.3 it states explicitly that those who have qualified teacher status must be able 'to assess pupils' progress accurately using, as relevant, the Early Learning Goals, National Curriculum level descriptions, criteria from national qualifications, the requirements of Awarding Bodies, National Curriculum and Foundation Stage assessment frameworks or objectives from the national strategies. They may have guidance from an experienced teacher where appropriate.'

USING LEARNING OBJECTIVES IN RECORDING ACHIEVEMENT

So far, the emphasis in discussing learning objectives has been on their formulation in the planning process, and then on their delivery in the teaching of a lesson or sequence of lessons. There has been some mention of their use in evaluating the success of lessons by the teacher: both self-evaluation and external evaluation. Now the time has come to shift the emphasis to their role in recording outcomes for students.

Record-keeping can be a sensitive topic for teachers. The increase in paperwork and meetings over recent years is a bone of contention in the profession. However, the issue of recording has to be grasped.

All teachers, as part of their professional activity, have to record the work and progress of students: from nursery to PhD level this is *sine qua non* of the business of teaching. No teaching can be effective unless the teacher understands the prior achievements of the learners: and the widely-claimed 'instinct' and 'gut-feeling' are not professional concepts (least of all in an age of accountability). Exactly when recording is done is for school managements and for teacher unions to decide. Let it simply be stated here that there is, and can be, no escape from the process if teaching is to be credible. So what are some of the factors which cling to the business of making those inevitable records?

In my own view there are five key questions which have to be answered for any kind of record keeping:

- What to record?
- How to record it?
- Where to record it?
- For what audiences?
- How often?

These are questions which have to be on the agenda of school management and staff meetings. There are statutory obligations to be met; and there are issues about in-school accountability too, for example of teachers to heads of department, to headteachers, to parents and – perhaps most importantly – to students.

In addition to these issues, there are matters of evaluation and review: and these are internal school matters. They can be summed up like this:

- Teachers need systems with which to review their own practice.
- Faculties/departments/year groups need to review their collective practice, too.
- The data on which these reviews take place need to be both qualitative and quantitative.

What does all this mean?

Recording student progress

At the level of the classroom, there have to be in place recording systems which tell the teacher and the student how students are performing. At the simplest, such a system consists of some form of marking/grading of on-going work, the results being recorded in a mark-book. This was the warp and weft of professional activity for many years: so long as there was a string of marks for each student/class each term, everyone was happy. Only rarely were questions asked about the significance of the marks, i.e. what they actually meant, or indeed what they represented in learning terms.

But what are the alternatives? On the level of recording as a process, the whole thing can be made to look more sophisticated these days by putting the data onto computer: but this does not guarantee increased meaningfulness!

The simple truth is that we all need to look more carefully at a variety of assessment techniques, so that what we record has real meaning in terms of the thinking students are asked to do. If, as many teachers claim to believe, SATs are inadequate because they measure only a limited amount of what is learned in the classroom, and they are mechanistic in their operation, then the profession has to come up with alternatives to supplement in-school recording and compensate for the inadequacies of SATs. To this end, you might like to try Activity 7.

Activity 7

Evaluating assessment methods

Below is a list of just some of the more usual and unusual methods of assessing student work.

In each case undertake an analysis of the advantages and the disadvantages of the method. Try to find at least three advantages and three disadvantages for each method. Add any methods of your own not listed here.

When you have done this, look over the result. Make a judgement about an appropriate situation in which to use each of the methods.

Try out your conclusions in your own classes.

Method	Advantages	Disadvantages	Used most appropriately to:
Teacher marks set work			
Self-assessment by students			
Peer assessment (students mark each other's work)			
Periodic tutorial review			
Personal target setting			
Students use reflective log: (What have I learned this week?)			
Other methods			

The Activity has, hopefully, focused your mind on the fact that a range of assessment methods can be used, all of them productively in appropriate circumstances, and that most teachers could broaden their range of assessment techniques. But assessment has to be set against criteria: and those criteria have to include or relate to the learning objectives which have been set for the lesson/session/term, etc. This can be illustrated by looking at a single assignment set to students, to explore how the process works.

An example of learning objectives linked to a student assignment: using pre-agreed criteria for assessment

The next point is an important one: many teachers do set learning objectives for lessons – but they miss out on a vital step in the process. They forget to tell the students what they are!

This is a point well made in the Draft Handbook (para 3.3.3) which says that teachers should:

● share planned learning intentions with pupils through discussion, display and, where appropriate, by encouraging pupils to note the learning intentions on their written work;

- encourage pupils to develop their own sets of success criteria for tasks (for example by asking, 'How will we know that you have achieved that?');
- teach pupils to use response sheets to assess their own work against the success criteria identified;
- share individual, group and class targets with pupils;
- teach pupils to identify and set their own next learning targets;
- teach pupils to evaluate their own work and progress.

Achieving learning objectives is best accomplished through a partnership between teachers and students. This can mean that, at the beginning of a lesson, the teacher spells out the objectives which it is hoped will be achieved by the end. In relation to a specific piece of work, these learning objectives can be set down as criteria. The criteria then become, effectively, the 'marking grid' against which the work is judged.

Figure 3.4 sets out one such task set to students in which the learning objectives have been converted into criteria for judging the work.

The task:

For many ordinary people in Victorian England life was sordid, dangerous and uncomfortable. Yet one book on the period was called 'The Victorian Achievement'.

What exactly were the achievements of the Victorian era? How significant have they been in shaping later events?

Criteria
1 **You must show a knowledge of the period and its aftermath.**
2 **You must have a coherent 'thesis' or line of argument.**
3 **You must weigh evidence about the importance of people/events, etc.**
4 **You must make reasoned judgements.**
5 **Your English should be readable and persuasive.**

Figure 3.4

An example of pre-agreed criteria for an assignment in history

Activity 8

Turning learning objectives into criteria for judging students' work
Examine the example set out in Figure 3.4.

If this is a technique which you do not use already, prepare some work for students in which you use this technique to supply them with a clear set of task instructions that includes the criteria for judgement.

Allow students to complete the task. Assess their performance.

Did the technique help them to focus their responses to the task set? Did they do better than you might have expected? In what ways? If not, why not?

Metacognition

It would be wrong to leave the topic of student assessment against learning objectives without some reference to metacognition. This is a rather high-sounding term for the process whereby students reflect on their own learning: *what* they have learned and the processes by which they learned it.

This is a technique which I have seen used effectively with students as young as Year 1 – so it is definitely appropriate for all the students whose performance is covered by this volume. But, it does require a bit of explanation from the teacher, and some training of students to help them to do it well.

At Key Stages 2 and 3 students can write adequately, so the best approach is for them to keep a written log. The teacher simply puts aside about 12 to 15 minutes a week for the log to be completed (it can be homework time rather than class time).

The teacher first explains that people learn better when they are conscious of learning. So students are invited to reflect on the week's learning. They can begin from quite easy questions (these can be duplicated and pasted into the front of the logs as reminders):

- What learning did I enjoy most this week? Why?
- What learning did I least enjoy? Why?
- What is it that I find difficult about some topics?
- What kinds of teaching help me to learn best?

They can then proceed to more difficult questions:

- What patterns of study help me learn best?
- How do I remember things most effectively?
- What targets do I need to set myself for the next week/term?
- How well did I achieve last week's targets?

Over time, students' responses to this task become more insightful, and therefore more valuable to them and to the teacher. Consider the following three responses to completing a log, and you can track the process at work.

Example 1: Year 4 student, new to the process

> I liked the work we did on the Greeks. It was interesting. I did not like maths. It's boring. I like story lessons.

Example 2: Year 6 student, with experience of keeping the log

> I enjoyed pretending to be a Roman soldier and the dressing up. I would have been good at bossing people about. I was afraid the new maths we did was going to be hard because it is called algebra. But it was like a game really, just finding the missing clue – good fun. I like learning things in groups like that best, and I have got less

> *scared about maths so I do it better. I need to write neater because the numbers sometimes get jumbled.*

Example 3: Year 9 student, with experience of the log

> *This new history topic is difficult because it asks you to collect your own information. I have had to give up one day's football after school to go to the library. I can do my other homework with Radio 1 on in the background. But this history I have to have silence for – so I got up very early and did it before anyone was awake. It was worth it – I got a B plus.*
>
> *Last week's target was to memorise the order of the battles: very hard! But Mr Smith taught me how to use a mnemonic and now I can do it.*

Metacognition and the teacher

The value of this process does not stop at the student: the reflective learning log gives the teacher vital clues about what is happening in students' heads. Regular review by the teacher of what students have written in their logs is crucial. In a study of metacognition in a primary class, Wilding concludes:

> *Developing metacognition is a key element in maximising children's learning. However, it is an equally important element in maximising teachers' own professionalism and quality of pedagogy – teachers need to be aware of the processes of thought that underpin their classroom practice if they are to be in control of it . . .*

and she goes on, teachers have to ask themselves, through this process:

> *Is what I am doing related to what I wanted to achieve? Are the children learning what I intended? How do the children respond to the activity? Is it justifiable as an effective way of achieving my learning aims?*
>
> (Wilding, M. (1997) 'Taking control: from theory into practice',
> *Education Today* 47.3, p. 23)

So once again, learning objectives appear at the very centre of the learning process, both guiding the students' achievement and revealing the teacher's effectiveness.

LEARNING OBJECTIVES AND TARGET SETTING: A NOTE

There is probably a degree of ambiguity in the statements that are made about target setting in many of the educational books and government statements that one reads. This is because the descriptor 'target' is used in two ways. The first seems to be demonstrable from the National Standards.

In para 3.1.6 of the Draft Handbook it requires teachers to be able to contribute to teaching teams and plan for the deployment of adult support for special needs pupils, and to link the work clearly to the targets set for individual pupils or groups of pupils. In this case, the 'targets' seem to refer to those intentions identified in Individual Education Plans. In the Draft Handbook para 3.1.2 reference is made to learning targets for classes, i.e. what we have called learning objectives.

However, in the Government's Circular 11/98 Target Setting in Schools, there is another use of the word, i.e. to indicate statutory targets. This Circular set out the legal position for target setting in and by schools. In summary it says:

- Target setting has been shown to help raise the standards of pupil performance.
- Maintained schools including special schools have to set statutory targets once a year.
- These targets must reflect the government's priority of raising standards in literacy and numeracy.
- The targets are set by the governing body of the school during the annual cycle of school review.
- Targets must be published.
- The LEA has a role in ensuring the targets set are realistic and challenging.
- At Key Stage 2 targets are construed to relate to the percentage of pupils reaching level 4 in English and mathematics.
- In the secondary sector targets relate to the percentage of pupils achieving 5 or more A*–C GCSE grades.

Oddly, the word target has disappeared from QTT (e.g. para 3.2).

Because of the problems relating to the achievement of pupils in special education, specific guidance is issued for special schools which allows the targets to be sub-divided into more manageable and measurable segments for these pupils – a process which is described in the guidance document *Supporting the Target Setting Process* (DfEE, March 2001).

The targets identified in Circular 11/98 are currently the only legally required targets; but schools are encouraged to identify targets of their own, for example in specific subjects or in areas such as multicultural education. In practice, many schools adopt non-academic targets, too: aspirations that relate to improving plant and buildings, facilities and so on.

Clearly, targets and learning objectives are not synonymous. In the academic or learning field identifying lesson objectives, or the objectives for a course or sequence of lessons, may (indeed, will) lead towards success with the broader issue of attaining the school targets. There is a relationship between learning objectives and targets that can be direct or indirect; and the teacher will need to be conscious of targets when formulating objectives.

The Government's White Paper, *Schools achieving success* (DfES 2001), states the official view (para 2.3):

Clear targets have been established and schools and teachers have better evidence available to enable them to evaluate their performance and are increasingly ready to challenge themselves to improve.

This is part of the accountability programme of government. The statement omits any mention of the debate about whether setting narrow achievement targets (like prescribing curriculum too closely, as some would argue the National Curriculum does) makes for a less effective education for children. This is a debate that teachers need to have, but which is beyond the present scope.

However, the White Paper does go on to point out that while fewer schools are falling into failure (para 2.4), and teachers in the primary sector have achieved a great deal (para 2.9), there is much work still to do at Key Stage 3 in particular (para 3.2). Readers who want to pursue the research grounds on which this assertion is based would do well to read the article by Michael Barber, a government adviser, which is referenced at the end of this chapter (Barber 1999).

Outcomes

In this chapter you should have:

- Gained a deeper understanding of the factors that affect classroom climate, and that have an effect on the intellectual ethos of classrooms
- Considered ways in which you can turn your learning objectives into learning outcomes, capable of assessment of varying kinds
- Looked critically at the issue of recording outcomes from pupils' work and progress
- Considered the links between learning objectives and targets, and how these complement each other in the classroom.

Barber, M. (1999) 'Taking the tide at the flood', *Education Today* vol 49.4, pp. 3–17.

REFERENCE

4 THE NATURE OF CLASSROOM TASKS

OBJECTIVES

This chapter invites you:

- To consider the definition of classroom tasks
- To realise the nature of classroom task setting as a key teaching skill
- To begin to understand how classroom tasks can be categorised
- To examine the relationship between effective tasks and cognition.

DEFINING CLASSROOM TASKS

In the first three chapters of this book we have looked at the formulation of learning objectives. The point was made that these are achieved through what the teacher goes on to teach or asks the students to learn. They can be achieved through the materials the teacher presents verbally (explaining), through the things the teacher asks (questioning), or through the work the teacher asks the student to do (task-setting). The first two of these skill areas have been dealt with in a companion book in this series. Here the emphasis shifts to the third skill: that of task-setting.

What exactly are classroom tasks?

My own definition of a classroom task is anything a teacher asks a student to do in order to promote learning. Some examples make the point.

- In English – to compose a letter seeking a job interview.
- In mathematics – to undertake a page of examples.
- In science – to conduct an experiment.
- In history – to collect evidence from several sources.
- In geography – to find the way round an orienteering course.
- In drama – to participate in a role play.
- In RE/DT – to model a biblical house.
- In PE – to gain a new skill in athletics.
- In IT – to operate an unfamiliar program.

The fact is that – in class, or for homework to bring back to class – all teachers set an array of tasks every week; and all students are on the receiving end of a battery of different kinds of task every week. The purpose of the next four chapters is to give you the opportunity to reflect on the process of task-setting with a view to improving this aspect of your work.

Guidance about, and even mentions of, classroom tasks are less frequent in official documents than are most other aspects of teaching skill. There seems to be an implicit assumption that this is such a basic technique that it needs little discussion and analysis. The present text would question that view.

What guidance there is tends to be oblique. It is assumed that tasks will be differentiated (see the later chapters of this book). Tasks are subject to learning objectives, which were dealt with earlier. They may have a role in assessment (Draft Handbook para 3.1.1). Tasks are seen as incremental; that is, they advance learning from the current to a new level (Draft Handbook para 3.1.2). Tasks may relate to a variety of different teaching styles or methods such as visual and movement activity, problem solving, using ICT or revision (para 3.1.3). Tasks may require resources, and teachers have to acquire skills in preparing and handling these (para 3.1.4). In fact one has to wait until para 3.2.1 of the Draft Handbook to get a specific mention of the role of tasks in the classroom. Here it is recorded that teachers must be able to demonstrate an ability in:

The selection and presentation of relevant and challenging tasks appropriate to age and current level of attainment.

In the primary sector teachers (Draft Handbook para 3.2.2) must:

Provide lively, structured activities to promote reading, writing, phonics and handwriting.

Tasks, then, are integral to classroom practice, but no guidance is outlined on how to organise them well, though there is an implication that tasks have a basis in cognition or thinking, and that this must feature in their planning.

Hay McBer is only marginally helpful, too. Effective lessons, we are told, are where little time is wasted (para 1.2.4), and expectations are high. Tasks may have a context in individual or small group work (para 1.2.7). Tasks are mentioned in the context of assessment (para 1.2.10) and homework (para 1.2.11).

QTT is cursory. NQTs will 'teach clearly structured lessons ... which make learning objectives clear to pupils'; but there is no mention of tasks themselves (QTT para 3.3.3).

The failure to deal in any detail with such a critical area of teaching skill as the ability to formulate classroom tasks that have real value to students is a major weakness of official guidance and seems to represent a lack of understanding of how classrooms really operate.

What kinds of task do teachers set?

The list on page 42 has answered this question at a superficial level. But in this section I want to explore the question more deeply.

In a companion book in this series I argued that teachers spend a lot of time talking and asking questions. It was suggested that the intellectual demand of these activities was variable: another way of expressing this might be to say that these processes had a variable ability to promote meaningful learning objectives. The argument went on to say that improvement in the quality and intellectual demand of teachers' explanations and questions would improve learning for all students: it would raise the intellectual climate of the classroom. The same argument applies to classroom tasks.

To explore this further I carried out an extensive piece of classroom research some years ago. Since then I have revisited this research periodically to see whether things have changed. Frankly, they haven't! So it seems appropriate to discuss some of the insights into tasks and task-setting which were gained from this research.

What research can tell us about tasks

The problem my researchers and I set ourselves was to try to discover what kinds of intellectual demands were made by the tasks which teachers set to students. Our contention was that, if learning is fundamentally about the quality of thinking and understanding which students engage in, then the tasks teachers set should reflect that cognitive demand. To establish the extent to which this situation applied in the early years of secondary schooling we picked a number of schools at random and sat in on lessons across a range of subject areas. Later we extended the research by gathering data from the primary sector, and from a wider range of school types. From this experience we were able to develop a huge collection of task descriptions (along with examples of the ways in which students responded to the tasks). These task descriptions were then scrutinised to see whether they fell into any patterns and, if so, what those patterns were. We found we could classify classroom tasks under some fairly clearly defined headings.

The first broad categorisation was quite straightforward:

- Low order tasks
- Higher order tasks.

These labels refer to the amount of thinking, or cognitive demand, the tasks made. Let us look at some examples.

A typical low order task would be:

When you write in your notebooks I like you to have a margin on each page. So that you don't forget, we are going to spend the next ten minutes going through notebooks so that you can draw the margins on now – on every page.

By contrast, a higher order task might be:

Over the last couple of weeks we have read a number of short stories together, and you have done some analysis of what you think makes them effective. Now it is your chance to use that analysis to write a short story of your own ...

Clearly, one of these tasks is more demanding than the other in terms of students' intellectual engagement. An objector might interrupt here, though, and say that the basic manual chores of classroom life have to be carried out. This is true: but they take up learning time. So – without putting ideal figures on teacher performance – a general conclusion might be that the greater the proportion of higher order tasks to low order tasks, the more learning might be happening in that specific classroom. In assessing task demand this quite simple dichotomy is really a very useful tool. Activity 9 asks you to do just that for some recent tasks you have set your own students.

Activity 9

Assessing the cognitive demand of your classroom tasks
Look back over the tasks you have set to students over the last term.
 Use a simple grid to classify these into higher order (H) or low order (L):

Task	H	L
Tables test		✓
Imaginative poem	✓	
(and so on)		
Total	x	y

Now take stock of the result – a percentage measure is quite useful: number of higher order tasks x 100 divided by the total of all tasks, or 100x over x + y.
 What does this exercise tell you about your own task-setting behaviour?

The results of this exercise are actually very crude, for reasons which we shall go on to explore.

Refining task definitions

One of the reasons why your analysis of task-setting in Activity 9 may be crude is that it is probably incomplete. If you looked back over students' written work, for example, you may have missed a lot of other tasks which you set during lessons for which there was no record. For our researchers, this situation did not apply. They sat in on lessons and recorded every task as it happened, so none was missed. The picture which emerged from this exercise was a complete one. This latter methodology probably picks up more of the low order tasks, and these proved to be enormously varied in nature. Table 4.1 sets out the variety of low level tasks which were noted – all of them more than once – and which were formed into sub-categories of low order task-setting.

 So, low level tasks tend to be about repeating old ground, about activities which are highly mechanistic, or they relate to work which is not designed to promote learning.

 Of course, some will say that these processes have value – and they may. Planning for a shy student to carry out an errand (type L2), with a

Sub-category	Description
L1 Disciplinary	Given as punishment, e.g. do extra work at break
L2 Administrative	Moving classroom furniture; running errands
L3 Drawing or colouring	Colouring in photocopied worksheets
L4 Copying	Usually notes from board
L5 Reading aloud	Usually around the class – level of engagement with material is ambiguous
L6 Silent reading or watching	Reading to oneself; watching a video, etc. Again, engagement ambiguous, but students often seen to be off-task
L7 Memorising	E.g. learning lists of dates
L8 Revising or taking revision test	E.g. spelling tests of pre-learned words
L9 Carrying out an experiment	If students merely repeated something demonstrated beforehand this rates low
L10 Simple comprehension	E.g. hear a story or historical event, then fill in missing words in worksheet
L11 Reinforcing	Repeating a skill already learned: e.g. in maths, learning a new skill and initial use of it = higher level, but after 250th example becomes low order, i.e. revision
L12 Looking things up	Category 12 was used to described looking up simple factual information; if the data was then used (not merely collected) this would transfer to higher order.

view to improving confidence, may have a value in the affective domain; but more often such tasks are unplanned and without intended purpose. Similarly it could be argued that less able students especially need to repeat work; and there is some truth in this. So while there is no absolute value judgement here, it is suggested that – as in Activity 9 – an eye needs to be kept on the erosiveness of low-level activities in classrooms and the negative effects this may have on students' excitement with learning.

If these are the low level tasks, we must pursue the question: what constitutes a higher order task? For this it may be helpful to look at how to categorise students' thinking skills. Such an attempt exists in the work of Benjamin Bloom. Bloom (1956) talked about high and low order thinking skills, just as we did (above). He was able to distinguish between those operations which required a minimal level of intellectual activity to achieve, and those which provoked depth of thought and understanding. In this context, 'rewarding' a student who has just got ten sums right with the task of carrying out another twenty almost identical calculations would engage the student in lower order thinking (practice, reinforcement). But to ask the student to take the learned skill and apply it to a new situation ('You have found the area of some of these rectangles; using squared paper can you find how to work out the area of this circle?') would be to require higher order thinking (in this case, application).

Bloom used this kind of argument to identify categories of higher

Sub-category	Description
H1 Imaginative tasks	E.g. creative writing; compose a haiku on the theme: Spring
H2 Collecting evidence, problem-solving, deducing, reasoning tasks	E.g. discover by experiment which substance melts soonest; what law or principle can you deduce from a number of similar maths problems?
H3 Application tasks	Take some given knowledge and use it. Also answers 'How?' questions
H4 Analysis tasks	Basically ask why? questions such as – why does it work this way?
H5 Synthesis tasks	Synthesis involves taking things learned in one situation and using them in quite a different one, e.g. using knowledge of block graphs in maths to illustrate something in history
H6 Evaluation tasks	'Write a review of this book'

Table 4.2

Sub-categories of higher order tasks set in classrooms

order skills, not so much into a hierarchy as into different types of process. The classification which was used in the research already referred to in this chapter drew on, but adapted, Bloom's work. Table 4.2 lists types of higher order task, and gives examples or descriptions of them.

Improving the cognitive levels of tasks

Too many tasks continue to be undemanding. Even during a period which I spent in the Further Education sector I was disappointed at the predictable and uninteresting, let alone undemanding, nature of much of the work. Copying from the board afflicted the lives even of 18 year-olds whose prime skill was not academic.

In the same way, when we studied the tasks set to accelerated examination sets working towards GCSE we found that, rather than becoming more intellectually demanding, tasks became increasingly banal. They were repetitive, involving much copying of notes and revision. They contributed little to a love of the subject studied, and nothing significant to a real understanding of it.

By contrast, tasks set to primary students tended to be consistently more demanding than those set in Key Stage 3. Why? Basically because, even in the post-National Curriculum era, many primary teachers devise work in a problem-solving format rather than allowing themselves to be totally content-dominated. This is a theme to which we shall return later.

So the key to task demand is in the nature of the tasks set: those characterised by Bloom's higher order thinking. Because this is so important, perhaps it will be beneficial at this point for you to practise recognising types of task. This, in turn, will help you to develop a mind-set in which you never compose a task for students without being conscious of what kind of a task it is. To this end you should now attempt Activity 10.

Activity 10

Practising task analysis

In Table 4.3 you will find 20 descriptions of real tasks which have been set to students in the early stages of Key Stage 3.

Use the task descriptions in Tables 4.1 and 4.2 to try to ascribe a subcategory (e.g. H1, L10, H3 etc.) to each of the 20 tasks.

Some of the tasks may seem very clear-cut. Others will be more ambiguous – perhaps due to the small amount of information you have about them. Enter into the debate with yourself and try to come to a decision.

When you have carried out the exercise you will find a commentary and set of suggested answers on pages 49–50.

Table 4.3

Twenty task descriptions for analysis

Tasks Sheet

1 'In front of you is a set of tubes, stands and vessels, and a small quantity of the chemical. You've just watched me carry out the experiment, now each of you set up your own apparatus and carry it out in your own time.' (**Science**)

2 'Before we start using this folder let's make it look neat. Go through each blank page and draw a margin on it.' (**Humanities**)

3 'Here is your written assignment for homework: what makes *The Diary of Adrian Mole Age 13¾* so compelling a book for such a wide range of readers?' (**English**)

4 'Right, in the small groups you've chosen, go into separate corners and prepare your play for showing fear.' (**Drama**)

5 We did this last week, so for homework it's page 33, examples 1–15.' (**Maths**)

6 'Here on the worksheet is the story I have just told you about life in Sri Lanka; but there are some words missing. Your job is to fill in the blanks.' (**Geography**)

7 'Imagine you are Hadrian. Where else could you have put the wall and why?' (**History**)

8 'I have shown you how to find the area of this shape. Now work out how you could find the area of this one.' (**Maths**)

9 'Here's the obstacle course. You have to go round in the shortest possible time. The route you choose is important. Think about it for a minute – then when I say "go" each person in turn . . . go!' (**PE**)

10 Write 10 good reasons why Britain is likely to become a nation of geriatrics if the present trends continue.' (**Social Studies**)

11 'Copy these notes from the board.' (**RE**)

12 When you've finished your story, illustrate it in any way you think appropriate.' (**English**)

13 'Each group take a map. Follow the trail marked on your group's map. If you get it right you will find a yellow card at each point marked X on the map. Collect 4 yellow cards and come back here in the shortest possible time.' (**Geography, outdoors**)

14 'First hand up: what has (1) eyes as round as saucers, (2) a head that can point backwards, (3) one ear higher than the other?' (**Environmental Studies**)

15 'In this video recording about the causes of unemployment, compare the strength of the argument put forward by the two politicians.' (**General Studies**)

16 (Round the class) '6 × 2?'
'5 × 4?'
'3 × 3?' (**Maths**) ☐

17 We are going to devise attractive back-drops for a disco. Think of the Chromatography you did in science. Now apply that principle to devise patterns that could be rainbows of colour but using a wider range of colours than in the rainbow.' (**Art**) ☐

18 'Devise a questionnaire to discover which of the television programmes are most commonly watched by pupils in this school, and what your fellow pupils' viewing habits are.' (**Social Studies**) ☐

19 'Look at page 15. Summarise in your own words the main causes of the French Revolution listed there.' (**History**) ☐

20 'Here is a poster showing a typical Palestinian house in about 5 AD. Using the card, scissors and glue supplied, make your own model of a house like this.' (**RE**) ☐

Raising the cognitive stakes in classrooms is an important part of the teacher's role, and should feature highly in the learning objectives for lessons. In this chapter we have looked at the contribution which task-setting can make to this process. In a further piece of research, undertaken in primary schools, I set out to look at the elements which could be incorporated into tasks (in this case, specifically tasks set in science lessons, though the principles apply across the curriculum) in order to ensure that students were being intellectually challenged. Table 4.4 identifies some of these elements.

Students can engage in . . .

- Affective activity – learning from one another
- Acquiring new mechanical skills
- Acquiring new information by their own efforts
- Experiencing a phenomenon or event
- Working from diagrams, plans, instructions
- Recording their own findings
- Memorising new technical data
- Identifying, e.g. specimens
- Estimating
- Guessing or hypothesising
- Analysing reasons or causes
- Testing hypotheses or concepts
- Formulating laws or generalisations
- Using evidence and drawing conclusions
- Solving problems
- Inventing new problems
- Evaluating situations and solutions
- Reporting orally and in writing

Table 4.4

Cognitive components in classroom tasks: some active elements

---

Commentary on Activity 10

Task 1 If this task is simply copying the teacher's lead then it is low order, L9. In some circumstances it could be made to have elements of H3, but nothing in the description confirms this

Task 2 Low order L3: this contributes nothing to learning as such, unless it is a deliberate attempt to improve the manual skills of small children

Task 3   An evaluative task – so H6

Task 4   This requires some imagination in conveying an emotion, and is higher order – H1

Task 5   Revision, L8

Task 6   The key is the words 'have just told you' – so this is reinforcement, L11

Task 7   A superb task involving elements of several higher order skills – H4 and H6 are strongest

Task 8   One assumes that the two shapes are similar so the task is Application – H3

Task 9   The shortest route has to be analysed, so H4

Task 10   The key word is 'why' – so H4

Task 11   L4 – there is no cognitive demand in this

Task 12   This could have overtones of H1, imagination; more often it is merely L3 – a device for keeping students of different abilities together

Task 13   This is an application task, H3, because the students must apply their orienteering skill to find the cards. Some teachers want to score this low because it does not require conventional classroom-based work: this is an error

Task 14   Problem-solving, using evidence and hypothesising: H2, elements of H6

Task 15   Evaluation, H6

Task 16   Almost certainly rote learning – L8, L11

Task 17   Transfer of scientific knowledge to the field of Art – i.e. synthesis, H5

Task 18   Strongly H2, though with overtones of other higher order skills

Task 19   'Summarise' suggests that this is a task which involves given/existing data, not the manipulation of data. This makes it low order, possibly L8

Task 20   The equipment is provided and the task seems uncomplicated copying as it is described: so L3. It could be made higher order if there are elements of technology incorporated into the task, but there is no evidence of this.

Outcomes

At the end of this chapter you should have:

- Understood how to assess the cognitive levels of the tasks you set
- Started to use this kind of analysis in your own preparation and teaching.

FACTORS IN EFFECTIVE TASK-SETTING

OBJECTIVES

This chapter invites you:

- To consider the factors that aid effective task setting
- To examine the role of exploring the learners' prior knowledge in making tasks effective.

EFFECTIVE TASK-SETTING

In the previous chapter we established that classroom tasks are things which teachers ask students to do, that they can be very varied in nature, and that they make varying intellectual or cognitive demands. In this chapter it is the intention to look at the skills the teacher needs in order to set effective tasks.

To this end, we can begin by looking at a list of prerequisites which help towards effective task setting.

Prerequisites for task effectiveness

An effective classroom task . . .

- has a clear purpose in the mind of the teacher;
- has a purpose which is communicated to the student;
- is couched in a form/language which is suitable for the target student group;
- is interesting;
- is of a cognitive level such as will stimulate and stretch the target students;
- is one of a series which will vary in form and demand;
- meets the needs of the target students;
- has clearly explained parameters.

Each of the items above is worthy of some discussion.

The task has a clear purpose in the mind of the teacher

This item need not detain us for long, since Chapters 1–3 of this book have laid down the processes for establishing the learning objectives for whatever it is that the teacher wishes to achieve. Just as lessons and longer-term sections of curricula need to be formulated alongside clear learning objectives, so each individual task within the scheme of work needs to be equally well planned.

The task has a purpose which is communicated to the student

But however well the teacher plans, that planning is only half effective if it remains in the mind of the teacher alone. To share learning objectives with students – and that includes the purposes for individual tasks – is to take a long stride in the direction of achievement of those purposes. Really good tasks are those in which the student begins with a clear sense of purpose. It is just like setting out on a journey: being lost on the back roads is fascinating on occasion, but most journeys have a purpose which cannot be achieved unless one arrives at the destination.

The task is couched in a form/language which is suitable for the target student group

In the same way, only tasks which are comprehensible are really likely to succeed. Effective tasks are couched in words which the students – all the students in the class – will understand; and the processes of carrying out the task must be clear. This means that tasks have to be explained clearly and good instructions given. At this point in the book the assumption is that a common task is being set to all students simultaneously. This is the commonest kind of task-setting, but later it will be necessary to deal with the implications of differentiation and dealing with ranges of ability within the task.

The task is interesting

This item should be self-evident. There is a growing body of opinion which suggests that students have a right to expect that teachers will make school work interesting: in some cases of high truancy, for example, it has been suggested that the key factor is a failure of interest caused by boring teaching. As professionals we have to take this view seriously: and it manifests itself, too, in the view that – since students have access to a range of media outside school, much of which is engaging to them – their in-school experience has to compete to survive. Even if neither of these arguments is, of itself, sufficiently persuasive to you, your own professionalism should require you to take the item seriously.

The task is of a cognitive level such as will stimulate and stretch the target students

Chapter 4 dealt with the details of cognitive level. Here the message is that tasks which make few demands rapidly bore students. Most students like a degree of challenge – even the least able like to feel that they are not simply time-wasting, or time-filling. The greater the degree of realism in the task, the more likely it is to capture the students' imaginations.

The task is one of a series which will vary in form and demand

For the same reason, over time, the tasks set by teachers need to vary in scope and style. Teachers, like others, tend to drop into grooves. X works well, so X becomes the staple diet of the classroom, and soon everyone is bored by X – first the students, but ultimately the teacher, too. Variety is, in that sense, the spice of life. Just as the serial story or the episodic soap opera presents a new and critical situation at each interval, so lessons have to have that flavour of freshness. This is demanding of the teacher, and needs attention to longer-term planning to bring it about.

The task meets the needs of the target students

Again, this sounds simplistic; but the fact is that research tends to suggest that only about half of all classroom tasks set are actually 'matched' to the level of need of the students. Thus too many tasks are either too hard or, usually, too easy for the target group. Differentiation, which is dealt with later, can help to solve this problem: but careful planning in the first instance, along with properly formulated learning objectives, may be a preventative step.

The task has clearly explained parameters

Finally in this short review of prerequisites we need to draw attention to the teacher's willingness to draw boundaries round the task. This will include such instructions as the length of time to take on it, the number of words to write, or the constraints to be put in place. For example, if the task were to compose a short play the teacher might limit it to four minutes' duration, on a prescribed topic, with three characters only. This item also includes indications to the students about the criteria upon which the task is going to be assessed. Such criteria should be stated 'up front', so that students are aware when working of what things require priority attention.

This short review of the prerequisites of task-setting has set the scene for you to have a look at your own practice using Activity 11.

Activity 11

Reviewing your own task-setting

Look back over the tasks which you have set for a term.

Use the items in the list on page 51 to assess how effectively you prepare for your own task-setting for students.

What items do you satisfy consistently?

What do you need to review about your own practice?

When you have completed Activity 11, look at the task example set out in Figure 3.4, page 37. This example (from a pre-GCSE class) picks up the final point above – about setting pre-agreed criteria, which then effectively become the assessment grid against which student performance on the task is judged.

TAKING STOCK OF THE TASK-SETTING PROCESS

So far, in the previous chapter and this one, the aim has been two-fold:

- to examine the nature of classroom tasks;
- to get you thinking about the skills you need to make your own task-setting successful.

At this juncture it is appropriate to deal with two other topics which are extremely significant in the task-setting process. These relate to the period before a task is set, and to the period after a task is completed by the class.

The learner's prior knowledge

Earlier in the chapter we looked at some of the prerequisites that make task-setting effective. One important factor was omitted there in order to give it individual attention: the learner's prior knowledge.

The basic thesis here goes like this. In order for a task to be effective it has to match the learner's current knowledge, understanding and skills; it has to meet the student's need and thus move him/her on on one or more of these fronts. Matching and meeting thus become twin principles for task-setting. However well formulated the task, and however interesting it might potentially be, it cannot succeed unless it matches and meets the student's current situation.

In practice, however, almost all task-setting is done without any systematic attention to this issue. Imagine two extreme but common scenarios:

- It is your first day with a new primary class, the first day of the Autumn Term. You may know the students' names, you may even have seen them carry out tasks (such as presenting an assembly) from time to time. But on what basis do you set the first tasks in those first few hours with the class?
- You are a teacher in Year 7 of a secondary school, and today you meet the children in your class for the first time. They have been drawn from eight different primary schools. You want to get on with the learning process and set them some homework; but how do you know what they have in common or of what any individual is capable?

Common enough experiences; and there are worse. For example, think of the plight of the supply teacher who meets a new class on every assignment!

What is needed is a strategy: a means for finding out what students know, understand and can do. Is it possible that research can help us here?

Certainly the literature of task-setting has some answers, so these need some scrutiny for what they might offer the teacher.

1 Diagnostic interview

This is a process whereby the teacher discusses aspects of the current learning at some length with each individual student in order to try to piece together the student's operational thinking and the understandings on which these are based. This is a useful method. The major drawback is time: in a normal classroom it would not be possible for a teacher to give each student enough attention to achieve this very often. However, properly applied, the technique is a good one. It can be used once or twice a year – for example, to establish students' prior knowledge at the beginning of a year, and progress and development at the half-way stage. It can be used with students with learning difficulties, especially where student–teacher ratios are favourable. It can be used with an individual student who has a learning problem with respect to a specific piece of work. The system of tutorial interviews, which is increasingly finding favour in the secondary sector, is built on this principle.

2 Word association and sorting tasks

This is rather a specialised approach, but it consists of presenting the student with a word to which he or she responds with the first word they think of. By repeating this process a trained operator (such as a psychologist) can establish whether a student is making connections between linked concepts. The method may have some clinical value, but is impractical for the classroom teacher.

3 Writing a definition

Another approach is to ask the students to write (or select from alternative) definitions which relate to the subject matter being taught. The teacher can judge from the definitions written (or the choices made) the level of sophistication of the students' understanding. This is useful in some circumstances and subjects (more so in science than in a foreign language perhaps), and has the advantage that it is a fairly economic process in terms of lesson time involved.

4 Testing

This is a very crude method for assessing prior learning. Most tests assess knowledge: but many educationists would argue that students become expert at simply listening to teachers and regurgitating acceptable answers. This process may lead to acceptable or better test scores, but it has little to tell us about the students' understanding. It is predicated on a view of knowledge as content and is inadequate as a professional activity.

5 Consulting records

One way with which to begin an assessment of students' prior knowledge is to read the records sent on from one class teacher to another, or from one school to another. There is a lot of research which suggests that this is rarely done! If the research is accurate, and it probably is, then one has to ask why records of this kind are compiled anyway. Clearly the answer is in terms of fulfilling the baser requirements of accountability rather than in terms of the furthering of any educational aims. But even where records are carefully compiled, are perceptive, and aimed at usefulness, they are often ignored.

It is common enough to hear the excuse that the teacher or school wants to assess the child for themselves and without prejudice. Phrases like 'fresh start' or 'clean sheet' abound. This attitude has a kind of spurious persuasiveness drawn from the rules of fair play about it – but it isn't really very professional. To read records does not mean that one has to be biased by them – objectivity is part of professionalism just as is avoiding prejudice. So records have some part to play in the process of informing teachers about students.

6 Feedback

In another book in this series it was suggested that teachers often use classroom questions to gauge students' knowledge, and so these questions form a kind of assessment of prior knowledge and current understanding. The value of this is not in doubt, subject to one important proviso: that the questions probe not just regurgitated content, but explore the students' mind-sets and the structure of their understanding and thinking. This brings the process closer to the diagnostic interview described above in point 1, but in a whole-class or group context rather than one-to-one.

Bowring-Carr and West-Burnham point to an important implication in the approach which has been described here. They note that assessing prior knowledge is to begin from where the student is. This is no new concept: the Plowden Report (1967) said exactly that. But Bowring-Carr and West-Burnham emphasise:

> ... *the culture of the school will have to change; it will need to change from one in which implicitly and explicitly the main emphasis is on enabling teachers to teach, to one in which the main emphasis is on enabling children to learn.*
>
> (Bowring-Carr, C. and West-Burnham, J. (1997) *Effective Learning in Schools*, London: Pitman, p. 106)

Some may feel that this view contradicts the fundamental basis on which a book on teaching skills is based: teaching skills are for teachers not learners! But I would challenge that view. Even Bowring-Carr and West-Burnham need teachers – though teachers redefined as the managers of learning. Such managers need 'teaching' skills: the facilitative skills which impart understanding to others. That is precisely what this book, and this series, is about.

So, from this chapter and the last, we have established that effective task-setting requires:

- the formulation of sound learning objectives;
- the systematic assessment of the learner's prior knowledge;

- the fulfilment of the prerequisites for 'effective tasks' described above on pages 51–53;
- the building in to tasks of appropriate cognitive demand;
- the establishment of pre-agreed criteria to indicate to students what will constitute success in tackling the task.

These steps lead us inevitably to look at the recording of student achievement once one or more tasks have been completed and assessed. Before tackling this next chapter, however, it may be valuable to take stock of your own approaches to assessing students' prior learning by undertaking Activity 12.

Activity 12

Assessing students' prior knowledge

In a paragraph or two, write a critical analysis of how you assess the prior learning of your students. Make sure that you answer the following questions in your analysis:

- What use do you make of
  - records from other teachers
  - testing
  - diagnostic techniques
  - other methods?
- How effective are the processes you use?
- How do you use the information you discover?
- What could you do to improve your techniques?

Now draw up an action plan for assessing the prior knowledge of students you encounter for the first time, e.g. at the beginning of the Autumn term or on starting a new job.

Though both the TTA (2001, 2002) and Hay McBer say little about task-setting techniques and skills, they are clear on one issue: that tasks have to be formulated in the light of the learners' prior knowledge. This is variously put, but most succinctly expressed in the Draft Handbook (para 3.1.2) which says that teachers must 'take account of, but reach beyond, pupils' present attainment'. This has been the overall message of this current chapter, and our intention has been to put flesh on the bare bones of the expectations in this area of skill.

Outcomes

At the end of this chapter you should have:

- Reviewed your own skills and techniques in assessing students' prior knowledge
- Practised some techniques for assessing the students' prior knowledge.

6 TRACKING AND RECORDING STUDENTS' PROGRESS

OBJECTIVES

This chapter invites you:

- To examine the issue of recording students' progress
- To look at the professional thinking that underpins the purposes and methods of recording
- To review the relationship between assessment and recording
- To examine marking and marking schemes in your classroom.

RECORDING ACHIEVEMENT: THE KEY QUESTIONS

With the task-setting process firmly established, attention shifts to the recording of the outcomes from the tasks. The following are the key questions which every teacher has to answer about recording students' achievements.

- Why record?
- How should the recording occur?
- What should be recorded?
- For what audiences are the records intended?
- Where are records kept?
- How often are they updated?

The following paragraphs take a first look at each of these questions; though it should be emphasised that schools and individual teachers need to answer the questions within their own contexts.

Why record?

The fundamental reason for recording is so that the progress of each student can be tracked. There are other reasons, too.

- So that teachers can assess whether learning objectives are being met;
- So that there is feedback to the teacher about the effectiveness of lessons, e.g. whether content is explained clearly and is understood;
- To inform future planning.

Ofsted inspectors are specially primed to look at this last point. They try to assess, in every lesson, whether feedback to the teacher is being used to inform what is happening in the short term and to influence future lesson intentions. Other implicit reasons for gathering assessment data are covered in the sub-sections that follow.

For the moment we need to pause over the factors that have given assessment and recording a poor press with teachers over recent years. These have been related to the controversies which have been generated about a) whether students are making better or worse progress now than in previous generations, and b) whether crude test results can be used as data against which the effectiveness of schools can be measured. In a book of this nature it is, perhaps, important to take a stance over each of these.

On the first, it is almost impossible for anyone, however well or badly motivated, to make a judgement. In times gone by, many students left school very early, or hardly attended. There is plenty of evidence of gross illiteracy and poor mathematical performance among youngsters and adults from the First and Second World Wars, for example. In our present environment some educationists would argue that the average school student has to learn much more in quantity, and a far wider range of knowledge, information and skills; so the fact that some fail to do so effectively is inevitable. Let us be clear: there is no room for complacency here. But a fifteen-year-old of today is unlikely to be less 'educated' than a fifteen-year-old of times past. That does not mean that the eleven years of statutory education have been well spent or successful; it simply means that comparisons are meaningless: the student of 1890 may have written in a fine copperplate but didn't have to master the Internet. The root question is: are we doing all we can, as well as we can, to equip all our citizens for life in the twenty-first century?

On the second issue, that of published results, for example SATs and GCSE results, there are quite blatant crudities in the system. Clearly, schools do not all start at the same point: facilities and buildings vary, the socio-economic climates of communities differ, the expectations of parents vary from one place to another and so on. To pretend that these factors are not significant is unintelligent. To suggest that it is only a matter of trying harder that will equalise the performance of all schools and of all students is ludicrous. But there should be measures of how well schools and students are improving. To demand and monitor these is reasonable; to use them as objective measures of success and failure without contextual information is facile.

For the teacher in the classroom, recording is a tool of the trade providing a source of feedback both to the teacher and, critically, to the student.

How should the recording occur?

Teachers need written, objective records to which they can refer. But this does not mean that a single standardised system of recording can be adopted to meet every contingency. Back in the old days, when I began my teaching career, schools were equally concerned with recording: but the records consisted of a string of marks out of 10 or out of 20 for items not clearly identified, with occasional percentages for end-of-term examinations. This system was neat, provided plenty of comparative statistical data, and kept everyone happy; though it was largely meaningless!

Records of performance can take many forms, and the simplest way of illustrating this is simply to list some and to let you, from your experience, add to the lists.

- Short accounts of diagnostic conversations with the student.
- Marks for periodic revision tests.
- Scores and/or comments against performance criteria for specific tasks.
- Mock SAT scores or exam results.
- Progress on National Curriculum Attainment Targets.
- Examples of specially interesting work or work which illustrates a student's difficulties (e.g. a page of work with b, d, p written backwards).
- Student self-assessments (about which more will be said later).
- Analyses of the student's cognitive achievements on specific tasks.
- Teacher summaries about students' knowledge, understanding. and skill levels.
- Notes, for example about a student's particularly interesting oral contribution to a lesson.

You will note that the emphasis in this list is not about scores, it is about teacher analysis of student performance: an important distinction.

What should be recorded?

The answer to this question is implicit in the previous sub-section: anything and everything that is relevant to understanding the ability and performance of each individual student.

For what audiences are the records intended?

The prime audience for records which track student progress is the ... student. This is certainly a very different answer from the traditional one ... the teacher. Both, of course, are important: but if the teacher is the facilitator of learning, then it is the learner who is at the heart of the recording process.

But, there are other audiences too. In an age of accountability, the teacher needs records in order to satisfy a number of people with legitimate reasons for knowing what the records reveal: the parents, the headteacher, other members of the department in a secondary school, colleagues in a primary school, teachers to whom students are handed on (on moving home or school), inspectors. The form of the recording may vary slightly from audience to audience, but this will be partly for the school to adopt a policy on.

Where are records kept?

The first answer is: securely. Records are confidential and should not be left on view. They need to be locked up or, if on database, then concealed with a code. Written records should not be thrown into skips or wastebins, but shredded; and certainly never left revealed on the car seat in the staff car park! Again, there should be school policies on these matters.

How often are they updated?

While records are distinguished by quality not quantity, there should be enough recording by individual teachers to ensure good knowledge of each student. Schools, including departments or year groups, will have rules and policies about what is an acceptable minimum.

To summarise, we might cast an eye over what government documents say about the value of assessment and the recording of progress and achievement. The collected wisdom seems to be:

ASSESSMENT AND RECORDING

- are at the heart of the learning process;
- support continuity between teachers, classes, schools;
- identify progress made by students;
- feed back to strengthen curriculum and teaching;
- help in future planning;
- improve student learning through feedback;
- should be part of the teaching/learning cycle.

This is a good moment at which to review your own practice in recording by carrying out the task in Activity 13.

Activity 13

Reviewing your recording systems

Revisit the issues discussed above, and try to evaluate the extent to which your recording practices are effective.

- Why do you record? Have you a clearly articulated policy? Has the school a policy? Are you fulfilling it?
- How does the recording occur? How systematic are you about your recording?
- What do you record? Is the range sufficiently varied? Does it take account of the students' perceptions of their progress?
- For what audiences are your records intended? Have you systems that allow you to meet the demands of each audience?
- Where are your records kept? Is confidentiality ensured?
- How often are your records updated?

Try to find an opportunity to share your ideas with one or more colleagues, and see what you can learn from their practice.

RECORDING ACHIEVEMENT: SOME ADDITIONAL ISSUES

The previous section of this chapter established the basic guidelines for recording students' progress. But a number of other matters are worth some discussion before leaving this subject.

1 Marking work

Good marking practice demands that the teacher brings to the process some sympathetic skills. Most marking will probably take place away from the classroom, but sometimes it is useful to mark alongside the student so that the student can gain an insight into the process and can have the immediacy of being able to see and contribute to the marking process. Marking should always be done within a reasonable time: it is useful to have a consistent rule about this such as 'Homework handed in each Monday, work returned each following Monday'. Nothing frustrates students more than work which is turned around slowly. Work must always be marked: failure to mark is culpable and a denial of professionalism. A good rule might be: set less work and mark it effectively rather than more work and skimp the process.

Commenting should always contain a reference to strengths as well as weaknesses – and guidelines for future improvement. Personally, given a choice, I prefer to write comments at the end or on a separate sheet rather than deface the student's work. In the primary school in which I work we have a system of comment sheets for major pieces of work such as the termly project (see Figure 6.1). This is exactly the same pattern as is used for my MBA students in the university (Figure 6.2). Comment sheets should be based on the criteria agreed for each piece of work (see below).

The Draft Handbook (para 3.3.3) makes pertinent demands on the teacher to:

- provide clear feedback to pupils through marking strategies; using marking (either carried out in the presence of the pupil, or as a written assessment to be read later by pupils) to:
  - highlight attainment (what has been learned)
  - recognise and reward effort
  - identify specific improvements (for example in handwriting or spelling)
  - encourage pupils to self-evaluate and assess their work
  - construct the way forward by identifying strategies that could develop and improve future work.

2 Pre-agreed criteria

On page 37 (Figure 3.4) the issue of pre-agreed criteria was discussed and illustrated. In recording student outcomes it is important to keep the marks/grades and comments for all the criteria, and not reduce the process to a global score which indicates little or nothing.

		Figure 6.1

Topic:	The Tudors
Main focus:	History. Focus of assessment: Elizabethan writing
Key issue:	Empathy (characters, events, feelings, understanding)

A sample of a comment sheet for a primary school project

English:	1 Speaking and listening
	2 Reading
	3 Writing
	• spelling
	• handwriting
	• presentation
	• overall success (purpose, audience, style)

Landmark assessments:	1 Story of a holiday adventure
	a) Punctuation, including dialogue conventions
	b) Overall success of the writing (in terms of purpose, audience, style)
	2 Story of exploration
	a) Punctuation
	b) Overall success

3 Self-assessment

From time to time it is quite reasonable to ask students to assess their own work. This may happen in a variety of circumstances or operate in several different ways. For example, a very able student may be asked to critique his/her own work: an exercise which stops the more able from skimping on quality. Or a whole class may use the answer-book to check their own maths exercise. This is a mechanical task which can save the teacher time – though the outcome still needs a professional eye to see what mistakes are being made and by whom!

Self-assessment helps to make students more responsible for their own learning, and is thus more appropriate for a twenty-first-century approach to learning.

4 Peer assessment

This needs careful handling, but should not be written off as a technique. One of the important lessons in life is that one's work and performance is judged by others; so it is vital to learn to handle that early in life. For example, in primary schools children sometimes swap books to mark work – rather like self-assessment except it is between partners. On a more sophisticated level, the teacher might ask students in a secondary design class to design a model according to pre-agreed

Student:	Date:
Title:	

Introduction	(title, scope, relevance, contents pages, outline research questions, order and rationale)
	_____/10____
Literature	(appropriateness, range, relevance, analytical treatment)
	_____/15____
Investigation	(appropriateness of methods, justification, execution)
	_____/15____
Analysis	(methods used, use made of data and appropriate manipulation, maximising outcomes)
	_____/25____
Conclusion	(effectiveness of 'drawing out the messages' and applying them to real situations)
	_____/10____
Presentation	(clarity of argument, layout)
	_____/10____
Overall	
	_____/15____
	TOTAL % GRADE _____

criteria and put the results up for scrutiny by the class. Some students will find this a painful process, and considerable skill is required of the teacher to protect the vulnerable.

5 Metacognition

This is a large topic, and has been dealt with earlier in the book.

6 Learning contracts

The use of learning contracts can be helpful in some circumstances. Reluctant learners may benefit from the security of knowing exactly what they have to do and when, and how the teacher will respond. I use a form of learning contract with less able youngsters in primary school. They are withdrawn from lessons for a period each week for additional help, but have to reinforce this time by undertaking some extra work at home. This extra work is assessed in the next withdrawal period. Some students find this a difficult discipline; but failure to conform to the requirement impedes the next withdrawal period and therefore their overall progress. In some cases I have had to form the contract both with the student and with a parent who agrees to oversee the work at home. The result is often increased interest from the home and improved performance by the student. If the work is effectively carried out there is often a small incentive in the form of a 'game' of some kind during the next session – though few of the students realise the 'games' are actually learning exercises in disguise!

7 Periodic tutorial review

In passing, it was mentioned earlier that some schools are now assigning students to tutors who sit down quietly with individuals and review progress from time to time. In a few schools, support staff or older students fulfil this role for younger pupils in place of teachers, and it seems to work effectively. Tutorial review means that someone is overseeing progress, and that adds an incentive to make some! In the context of review by a teacher, recording can be useful.

8 Reflective teaching

Finally in this review of issues in relation to recording, it is appropriate to mention the philosophy of reflective teaching. Reflective teachers scrutinise their own performance, including the lessons they learn through the tasks they set and how the students respond to these. Sometimes they do this using a written log of some kind; but even carrying out the Activities in this book of skills is a way of reflecting on your own teaching. Reflective teachers are those who thus continually review and update their skills, using practice and outcomes as the basis for moving their own professionalism on.

THE SKILLS REQUIRED OF THE TEACHER

Assessment and recording are key skills in the armoury of the teacher, and so it is not surprising to find that they feature significantly in the Draft Handbook for teachers. According to this document (para 3.3.1) teachers must be able:

> *To use and, where appropriate, to devise a range of monitoring and assessment strategies to evaluate pupils' progress towards planned learning targets, and use this information to improve their own teaching.*

There is some elaboration of this cluster of skills in the Draft Handbook document, all of which is pertinent, and to which you are referred (TTA 2001). To summarise, however, the following key issues are identified. In this context, one should read the word 'targets' to have a range of meanings:

- The learning objectives for a lesson or scheme
- The school's own statutory targets as discussed earlier in this manual, and
- The national targets for pupils at KS2, and at KS4 (towards which our KS3 students are working).

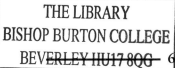

Assessment and recording have to illuminate the strengths and weaknesses of individual pupils, and in particular those who may be deemed to have any form of special need (including the more able as well as the less able). Attention must also be paid to matters such as gender and ethnic grouping, and their relation to performance as revealed through assessment (Draft Handbook para 3.3.5); and provision or recommendation must be made for support to be given to children with learning problems (para 3.3.6).

Insights gleaned from the assessment and feedback process must, inevitably, inform future lesson planning. Even more significantly, instant feedback (e.g. pupils' work on tasks monitored by the teacher) must be used during the lesson itself to change the teacher's strategies in line with the learner's needs. This is one of the factors assessed during the observation of lessons by Ofsted inspectors, and so it is of crucial importance that teachers master this rather subtle skill. Furthermore, provision of immediate oral feedback to pupils as they work is, rightly, seen as important – and this within a context of high expectations and good classroom climate. The Draft Handbook 3.3.3 refers specifically to teachers 'using assessments to involve pupils reflecting on, evaluating and improving their own performance', and so you might like to refer back to pages 38–39 where metacognition was discussed.

The Draft Handbook requires teachers to contextualise their assessment and recording against such criteria as National Curriculum level descriptions, criteria from national qualifications and data from sources such as the Panda reports supplied to schools annually (para 3.3.4).

Communication of the outcomes of assessment and recording practices to relevant audiences in writing or orally is an essential skill (Draft Handbook para 3.3.8). The same message appears in QTT paras 3.2.1–3.2.7 – these have been reviewed above. This chapter has, it is intended, moved the reader closer towards the understanding and skills needed to do these jobs effectively.

CONCLUSION

At the start of this chapter we had established that the following criteria are essential to effective task-setting:

- the formulation of sound learning objectives;
- the systematic assessment of the learner's prior knowledge;
- the fulfilment of the prerequisites for 'effective tasks' described above on pages 51–53;
- the building in to tasks of appropriate cognitive demand as described in Chapter 4;
- the establishment of pre-agreed criteria to indicate to students what will constitute success in tackling the task.

To these this chapter has added:

- the importance of marking work using a variety of techniques;
- the need to track student progress systematically through task responses;
- the need to communicate with students and others the outcomes of progress review;
- the need to think out ways of involving students in taking responsibility for their own progress;
- the need to develop oneself professionally through a reflective approach.

In the next chapter we move to look at task-setting in practice, and some examples of tasks for analysis.

Outcomes

At the end of this chapter you should have:

- Reassessed your approaches to assessment, recording and marking
- Overhauled your systems for recording
- Become more sensitive to the audiences for recording and feedback
- Thought out how to make students more responsible for tracking their own progress.

---

7 TASK-SETTING IN PRACTICE

OBJECTIVES

This chapter invites you:

- To consider a real example of task-setting at work in the classroom
- To analyse the example, assessing the strengths and weaknesses of the techniques used
- To think about the learning that went on in the lesson described
- To consider issues about tasks set in the specific context of homework.

INTRODUCTION

In the previous three chapters we have looked at the nature of classroom tasks and their cognitive demands, at the skills of setting effective tasks, and at assessing and recording progress through task-setting. In this chapter we look at an example of task-setting in action to try to work over the practical issues and problems. The task described is a real task which was actually used: and it could be set to any class in Key Stages 2 or 3 with minor adaptations of context and content, for example by adapting to a different lesson length or by changing the subject matter.

The task

Our teacher – we will call her Miss Smith – teaches in a small primary school. The students are divided into Key Stage 1 and Key Stage 2 classes, and Miss Smith teaches Key Stage 2. She has pupils in Years 3 to 6 in the same class, and the class is about average in size at 34 students. The classroom is just large enough for this class size: the students sit in fours, grouped round tables, with the exception of two students who are at a small table in a rather cramped corner. There is the advantage of a small work-space through folding doors which lead off the classroom, but this has to be used with care as students can disappear out of the teacher's eye-line.

The students have been studying Ancient Greece as part of the National Curriculum. Though the main thrust of the work has been historical and geographical, this theme has governed their work in English, RE, story-time and science as well. They have had a visit from a music specialist talking about ancient instruments, and from an architect who has explained some of the principles behind Greek buildings using specially-made build-it-yourself kits which the children could put together. The term and the theme are drawing to a close, and the teacher wants to draw together some of the threads of the work.

Miss Smith is also aware of some of the social factors which affect this class. Teaching across ages is not easy: and one constant need is to provide activities in which everyone can play a part and which cater for each student's level of maturity. There is also the intellectual issue: a four-year age-span also represents a myriad variations in intellectual ability combined with emotional maturity.

Miss Smith decides to dedicate the equivalent of a school day to the 'finale' of the Greek theme. But she feels that a whole day may be too long for some students: so she decides to use three of the four sessions on Day I (having begun the day, as is usual in this school, with some spelling and number work), plus a final session on Day 2.

This is the context. Now she has to decide on the task.

Miss Smith decides that the students should write a newspaper. One purpose of this task is that it draws together the work that has been done over the term. Another is that it contributes to the English curriculum by helping the students to identify audiences and to write in appropriate styles. The third consideration is that everyone, from Year 3 to Year 6 can contribute. Finally, she has a further learning purpose. For some time she has been concerned that the students do not work quickly enough, and with sufficient focus, unless she oversees them. She is concerned to develop greater self-motivation, and she thinks that the newspaper task can deliver this. This, then, is the basic plan.

Miss Smith decides that, of the four sessions available, she must spend a part of the first session sharing with the students what they have to do, and explaining the purposes of the task. She also needs some discussion time about the nature of newspapers, so that the students share the concept with her and each other. Her basic time-plan looks like this:

DAY 1	
Session 1:	Explain the task
	Talk about the nature of newspapers
	Get everyone started
Sessions 2 & 3:	Everyone working on a specific aspect of the newspaper
DAY 2	
Session 4:	The newspaper comes together.

GETTING STARTED

So Miss Smith is now ready for Session 1. She begins with an introductory talk lasting a few minutes in which she brings to the students' notice a local paper with a powerful headline. The children talk about the headline; and then Miss Smith goes on to ask about what else they could expect to find in newspapers. She elicits the kinds of answers she hopes for (features, advertisements, sports pages, pictures). They talk about who reads the paper, what makes it interesting, the style in which different parts are written, the kinds of pictures that are used and for what purposes.

She then goes on to ask what kind of newspaper might have been produced in Ancient Greece if the technology had been available: there were plenty of good observers and writers, so what would have the papers reported?

Finally, she moves on to newspaper production. Who writes? How are the pictures produced? Who puts the paper together? and so on.

The students are quite enthusiastic about all this, and they are excited when she says that they are going to produce their own paper.

It is thus a joint decision that the class feels it should write the paper for their parents – to display in the waiting area the next day for parents to read as they come to collect their youngsters from school. It is a joint decision, too, that not everyone can do the same job, so tasks have to be allocated. Miss Smith is appointed the Proprietor; and she has to appoint editors, reporters and so on.

A key factor to be stressed by Miss Smith is the time factor. Deadlines are explained. Now everyone is ready, and keyed up, to start work. All that remains is for jobs to be allocated.

Three older students are appointed editors: two for text and one for pictures. They have two roles: to choose the material to be included, and to fit it into the space available. (This is a manual process, since not enough computers are available to word-process the whole product: though some parts of it – such as the title page – will be produced using computers and duplicating facilities.)

A number of students are allocated to the advertising department; others to picture production; some to writing features; some as reporters. A couple are appointed cartoonists. Others become sports specialists. Deadlines are reinforced. The work begins.

After lunch, in Sessions 3 and 4, the work continues apace. The teacher is able to spend a lot of time monitoring individuals and their contributions, discussing content and style. The editorial staff have set up an office in the work-space next door. They have put a notice on the door which reads: 'Editors Office – knock to enter'. They are preparing the large sheets of paper on which they will make their layouts of the final designs for the paper and are working on producing the computer-generated title page.

The feature writers are having to think about what kinds of features, and what subject matter, they want to cover. The cartoonists are mocking up cartoon layouts and deciding on subject matter. The sports reporters are thinking up what they can say about Ancient Greek sporting events. The news journalists are trawling through what they know about Ancient Greece to find good copy for the front pages. Advertisers have to imagine what Ancient Greeks would find attractive to buy ... and so on.

As the afternoon goes on, things take shape and some features are beginning to emerge. The Proprietor has to remind the workforce about deadlines; and the editors have rejected some early copy because it isn't good enough! Commitment is high and the line between fantasy and reality is becoming blurred.

At the end of the day, the whole newspaper team comes together to take stock. The editors say what they still need. The Proprietor urges deadlines. Some pages are taking shape and can be shown and shared, but there is still a long way to go and only one session tomorrow in which to make the deadline. Everyone goes home with a few butterflies in the stomach – not least Miss Smith.

The next day is a fine one: that's good because poor weather makes the students fractious and today they have to concentrate. The pressure is building. The two text editors have their work cut out now receiving, judging, amending and spacing the contributions. The picture editor wants better material. The duplicator is playing up, but the headlines still need magnification on the copier. Everyone is struggling. As the session proceeds, the pages take shape. One or two students whose work has been rejected by the editors go away and produce something better because they don't want to be left out.

Just when she thinks she is winning, Miss Smith is approached by the text editors. They have a half-page blank and want her to contribute something within the next twenty minutes to fill the space! She has to sit at a word processor and write, against the clock. There are three minutes left to the end of the session: and the newspaper has to be published when the bell goes. They make it, but it's a close call! Spontaneous cheer.

OUTCOMES

Miss Smith has achieved her aim of getting a newspaper, and getting it by the deadline. Later she has time to take stock of precisely what the newspaper consists of. What follows here is a selection only of the contributions.

From the news section of the Athens Recorder:

Could it have happened?

A school in Athens has been attacked. Several children have been killed, and two teachers including the headmaster Helos Ancos. The Greek police have sealed off the area completely. Some of the children have given a description, a clear description.

Here is the description given by six-year-old Dephos Elios: Dark hair, dark skin, dirty, tall, slim build and big feet.

If you see him ring Athens 02132596. (Y5)

Kidnapped!

Yesterday a girl aged nineteen was kidnapped in the market. School children like Theseus King, Jason Sarjent and Timothy Ricket saw this terrible thing happen. They have explained that a black, dark man called Hades invaded the market. Beware! He will take your children. Demeter, Kore's mother, has put a terrible spell on Greece till she gets her child back … (Y4)

Gods

Yesterday Poseidon got angry and made an earthquake. Here are some witnesses' accounts of how it was.

Σαμ: It was terrible, you can't explain.
Ασλη: It was terrible. (Y3)

The Answer

A scientist called Archimedes has invented a screw to lift water up from one level to another.

I spoke to a farmer called Philippos who has used the Archimedes screw and this is what he said:

"It was very good for watering the crops. It was quicker. It was very good and I will use the Archimedes screw every day." (Y6)

The Trojan Horse

Today in Troy there was an accident and this is Elizabeth Richards reporting from Athens in Greece.

"It all started when the clever Athenians made a wooden horse and filled it with soldiers. The next day the Athenians pushed the horse to the gates of Troy.

"The Trojans thought it was a gift from the gods. So they pulled the horse into the city.

"That night the soldiers crept out of the horse and destroyed the city. So that was the end of Troy." (Y3)

From the theatre page:

Alexander the Great in Costume

Here at the best theatre in Greece you can watch one of the most important persons in Greece, Alexander the Great.

He is playing the part of a cruel, heartless king who would turn anyone away who came for help.

The character does not bring Alexander's true personality out, for Alexander is a kind, helpful person, the opposite of the character he is playing. (Y4)

Oh no it isn't!

Oh yes it is! A brilliant performance put on by Athens' best theatre.

The play they put on was about Kore, snatched by the evil god of the underworld. It was a great success, with the famous female actor Euripidia Annalayas as Kore, and the famous male actor Sophocles Annalayas as Hades. It was brilliant.

A few lucky locals were acting as villagers.

I asked one of the theatre-goers, who said: "It was excellent the way Kore screamed." (Y5)

TAKING STOCK

The purpose of describing Miss Smith's task and its outcomes at some length has been to give you, the reader, some basis on which to begin to make judgements about classroom tasks using a task other than one which you have invented yourself.

The task described above could have been used in a variety of subject areas, especially (but not exclusively) in the humanities. It could also have been adapted for use by students of any age up to the end of Key Stage 3.

What is important about the task is the extent to which it reveals the strengths and weaknesses of the task-setting. For this reason you might like to start by analysing the task against some of the criteria which were discussed in Chapter 5. To do this you can attempt Activity 14.

Activity 14

Analysing the effectiveness of Miss Smith's task

Read over Chapter 7 again using the criteria listed there and below to try to assess how effective you think Miss Smith's task-setting was.

Item	Positive features	Negative features
1 The task had a clear purpose in the mind of the teacher.		
2 The purpose was communicated to the students.		
3 The task was couched in suitable language for the target group.		
4 The task was interesting.		
5 The task had a cognitive level to stretch and stimulate the students.		

6 The task was one of a series, varying
   in form and demand.
7 The task met the needs of the students.
8 The task had clearly explained
   parameters.

Having established how effective this task was for its intended audience, you should think about issues relating to the cognitive demand of the task in a little more detail. Activity 15 will start you on this process.

Activity 15

Identifying the cognitive elements of Miss Smith's task
Look down the list below, which is taken from Table 4.4 (on page 49).

Use the items in the list to decide which cognitive elements were present (as far as you can judge from the evidence presented in this chapter) in Miss Smith's task.

Remember, evidence may be found either in the account of the task or from the ways in which the students interpreted it.

Component	**Present (✔)**	**Not present (✗)**
1 Affective activity		
2 Acquiring new mechanical skills		
3 Acquiring new information by students' own efforts		
4 Experiencing a phenomenon or event		
5 Working from diagrams, instructions, etc.		
6 Recording students' own findings		
7 Memorising new data		
8 Identifying, e.g. specimens		
9 Estimating		
10 Guessing or hypothesising		
11 Analysing reasons or causes		
12 Testing hypotheses, concepts		
13 Formulating laws or generalisations		
14 Using evidence, drawing conclusions		
15 Solving problems		

When you have completed the grid, ask yourself which of the missing components could and should have been built into the task.

Finally, tackle Activity 16.

Activity 16

Deciding on the cognitive level of Miss Smith's task, and recording the students' performance

Re-read the section about cognitive levels of tasks on pages 44–47. Then decide whether you rate this task overall a higher order task or a low order one. Perhaps parts of it fall into each category – if so, which parts are higher order and which low order?

Now consider the issues about recording discussed in Chapter 6. We are not told how Miss Smith recorded the outcomes of her task. How would you have set about this?

Before we leave the topic of task-setting it is important to examine critically one of the contexts in which task-setting frequently occurs: the homework setting.

HOMEWORK: A CONTENTIOUS ISSUE

QTT para 3.3.12 implies that teachers must know how to set homework – and that homework is set in order to consolidate classroom learning – a rather constrained view of its usefulness. Tasks set for homework, as opposed to tasks set for class work, are simply classroom tasks in a different context. There is no question that government guidance favours the use, and even extending the use, of homework – mainly as a way of extending school time. A range of government documents requires teachers to set, mark and use homework effectively. Indeed, when homework is set, all the strictures in this book apply to the process. However, just because something is a requirement – and we have to conform to it – does not free it from the rigours of public and professional scrutiny. To this end you are invited to read the Critical Review that follows. It is the review of a book published in the USA, but one that epitomises the debate. As you read you should carry out Activity 17.

Activity 17

Evaluating the pros and cons of homework

As you read the Critical Review of Kralovec and Buell's book, which follows, try to marshal your own thoughts about the arguments for and against the use of homework.

Ask yourself:

- How effective is homework as a learning tool? (Weigh its advantages and disadvantages)
- How could its use be improved?
- What better alternatives might there be?

The End of Homework

Etta Kralovec and John Buell
Boston, USA: Beacon Press 2000

A critical review

This review is written from a perspective of bias, so I will declare it from the start: I agree totally with the sub-text of this book that 'homework disrupts families, overburdens children and limits learning'. One could add 'and is socially divisive'.

This view may not be shared by all in either the UK or the USA. David Blunkett, fronting the Standards website for the former DfEE, said with all the authority of a (then) Secretary of State for Education:

> *A good, well organised homework programme helps children and young people to develop the skills and attitudes they will need for successful, independent lifelong learning. Homework supports the development of independent learning skills, so investigation and enquiry are seen as part of the learning process ... Homework partnerships with parents, carers and pupils are vital to extending high quality learning beyond the limits of the school day.*

The problem with this high-sounding rhetoric is that it is based, in my view, on uncertain evidence and some false assumptions. This review article will outline the problems and then go on to examine the contribution that Kralovec and Buell have made to the debate.

The ineffectiveness of homework and its potential to disrupt have long been recognised by sociologists of education, and pupils have always seen it that way as Meighan (1981), quoting Blishen (1969), reports:

> *Prefects, homework, bells and religious education all received considerable scorn. (p. 33)*

How slowly education responds! Thirty years on, prefects may be a dying breed but the other pet hates still hold majority sway.

But why does homework get such a bad press? Is it merely because it's a burden?

Perhaps that question needs to be rephrased. Imagine an adult going to work from 9.00–5.30, in an office, a shop or a factory. The time comes to go home and the boss announces two or three hours of compulsory unrewarded overtime to be done in the home before the next morning. Middle-class professionals may smile smugly and reflect that that is modern business; but the blue collar workers won't. Not only that, who is right? Do we, as adults, want a workaholic world? Even if we do, have we the right to impose one on our children? Homework is essentially unreasonable and unjust. It makes the assumption that school work cannot be done at school, that school is simply not a large enough part of life. If pupils are not learning cerebrally and independently in school what are they wasting time doing?

Part of the problem here is that school work is in considerable need of redefinition. In today's information world, even more in the knowledge world of the immediate future, what will be needed from adults (and to be learned by pupils) are the skills of handling that knowledge – refining it, reflecting on it, going through the cerebral processes. If those things are done in school, then they don't need to be an add-on for homework. If they are done at home, what is happening in school? In fact, there is evidence to suggest that too much homework is boring and ineffectual precisely because it fails to address the cerebral issues. Thus Bleach (1998), for example, records a recurrent theme that:

Many homeworks are mere continuations or leftovers. (p. 45)

But even if homework were assiduously set, and catered for the cerebral, it would still run up against a significant problem: the failure of equal opportunity. For every middle-class home that can afford to provide a quiet study for the pupil, a desk, computer, musical instruments and so on, there are a dozen or more homes (and conscientious parents even) that cannot. Homework may create inequality; it certainly exacerbates it, as it did for the failing working-class girls in Plummer's (2000) account:

The significant events in my life were family illnesses, a father temporarily out of work, the burden of too many domestic responsibilities ... (p. 164)

What price homework in surroundings like these? Belle's (1999) account of the after-school lives of children in America reinforces these findings.

It is in high-achieving, but high socio-economic status, schools where school hours can be extended by parental demand or connivance, and thus results improved comparative to less favoured social situations (Woods 1996), where the pressure for success comes from a few ambitious parents (Crozier 2000). But it probably comes at a price – the over-stressing of over-worked pupils.

The simple fact is that the evidence of the effectiveness of homework is inconclusive (Doyle and Barber 1990; Easton and Bennett 1990; Sharp, Keys and Benefield 2001). In a controlled study Kazmierzak (1994) apparently found that when, during the first quarter of the second semester with an experimental group of American students, homework was not checked by the teacher, pupils' quarterly grades were on average only one per cent lower than when homework was checked. Most detached observers of the homework scene suggest that 'homework' is effective only when it is carried out in a supportive situation (Sanacore 1999). Thus schools with homework facilities after the school day, schools with homework clubs, and schools where learning contracts (as opposed to the schoolwork/homework divide) are in operation, are more likely to be successful in encouraging effective learning through beyond-class tasks.

So what is the value of Kralovec and Buell's book to this debate?

The book is full of pertinent examples of how and why homework fails. It attempts to deal with the rationale that underpins homework and to criticise it in a logical, rather than politically emotive, way. It is based on research and literature, so the student of the topic can follow up the views expressed. It reviews the vast range of reasons as to why homework fails. It is salutary to list the main ones amongst these:

- Stress in the family caused by failure of the adults to help effectively with homework;
- Failure of relationships in families because of lack of time for one another;
- The increasing problem of physical injury to pupils caused by being weighed down with bags full of school chores and kit;
- The fear of failure if large quantities of homework are not set and completed;
- The failure of homework tasks to achieve useful learning objectives;
- The failure of teachers to mark and provide feedback on homework effectively;
- The underlying belief that homework is the only legitimate learning experience outside school;
- The exhaustion brought on by too many hours of working on similar tasks;
- The failure to understand that children need to be children;
- The naive belief that time management can be learned only through strict homework regimes;
- The failures of equity across cultures, religions and gender as a result of homework activities;
- The redundancy of homework in the new learning cultures of the information age;
- The fiscal failures to provide 'extended study' facilities for pupils suitable for beyond-school activities;
- The belief that academic success is the only success;
- The questionable position that fighting with one's children for twelve years about doing their homework fosters good habits in them;
- The frequent loss of interest in academic work fostered by excessive exposure to it through homework;
- The tendency for many pupils to cheat or copy, or otherwise subvert the homework system.

In the end, the book is an appeal to return to a values-orientated education world rather than one that sees 'standards' (and standards in a limited range of skills and abilities) as the only valid measure of value. It puts the child back into childhood, and the freedom back into democracy.

If there is a problem of lack of time in school it may not be an issue of extending the school day beyond reasonable limits with homework. It

may rather be a matter of revisiting the overloaded curriculum requirements, cutting down on mere information, and concentrating on
thinking and cognition more effectively in classrooms.

Like many of my generation I, too, suffered interminable homework:
two-and-a-half hours a night six nights a week at eleven, three hours
each night from the age of twelve until the age of eighteen. It was
basically extension work. Little of it cost the teachers marking time
because it was rehearsed in class. It had to be done in a poor, working-
class, single-parent environment largely lacking in either facility or
guidance. It was an intolerable burden in addition to the school day,
and two-and-a-half hours of travelling time daily. Between the ages of
eleven and eighteen one chose between punishment for failure and the
total destruction of any concern but school. It was inhuman then; and it
is inhuman now, which may have been why the California Civil Code of
1901 stated:

> *No pupil under the age of fifteen in any grammar or primary school
> shall be required to do any home study. (Quoted in Kralovec and
> Buell, p. 39.)*

References

Belle, D. (1999) *The after-school lives of children.* London: Lawrence Erlbaum
    Associates
Bleach, K. (1998) *Raising boys' achievement in schools.* Stoke on Trent: Trentham
    Books
Blishen, E. (1969) *The school that I'd like.* Harmondsworth: Penguin
Blunkett, D. (2001) The Standards Site. www.standards.dfee.gov.uk/otherresources/
    homework
Crozier, G. (2000) *Parents and schools: partners or protagonists?* Stoke on Trent:
    Trentham Books
Doyle, M. and Barber, B. (1990) *Homework as a learning experience: what research
    says to the teacher.* West Haven, CT: NEA Professional Library
Easton, J. and Bennett, A. (1990) *Achievement effects of homework on sixth grade
    classrooms.* Paper presented at the Annual Meeting of the American Educational
    Research Association, Boston, MA, April 16–20 1990
Kazmierzak, K. (1994) *Current wisdom on homework and the effectiveness of a
    homework checking system.* Indiana, USA: Indiana University
Meighan, R. (1981) *A sociology of educating.* London: Holt, Rinehart and Winston
Plummer, G. (2000) *Failing working-class girls.* Stoke on Trent: Trentham Books
Sanacore, J. (1999) *Needed: homework clinics for struggling learners.* ERIC source
    no. ED428325
Sharp, C., Keys, W. and Benefield, P. (2001) *Homework: a review of recent research.*
    Slough: National Foundation for Educational Research
Woods, P. (1996) *Contemporary issues in teaching and learning.* Basingstoke: Open
    University

This Review is reprinted by permission of the College of Teachers from
their journal *Education Today* vol. 52.1.

SUMMARY

In Chapters 4 to 7 an attempt has been made to look systematically at the factors which make teachers' task-setting effective, and at the demands which tasks make on students. A basic thesis of these chapters has been that task-setting is a skill which can worked upon and improved through a little focused thought and by incorporating an appropriate level of task demand for the student audience.

In the task example provided by Miss Smith (because she was teaching children of mixed ages and abilities) we were also moving towards a crucial topic which has not been dealt with explicitly so far in this book, but which is the subject of the next three chapters: differentiation.

Outcomes

At the end of this chapter you should have:

- Compared the task-setting skills in the sample lesson with your own
- Analysed the cognitive components of task-setting in more depth
- Rehearsed the arguments about tasks set for homework and reached a more sensitive understanding of this form of working as it affects pupils.

8

THE PURPOSE OF DIFFERENTIATION

OBJECTIVES

This chapter invites you:

- To consider the rationale behind differentiating classroom work
- To be aware of the skills required of the teacher to differentiate effectively
- To review some common strategies for differentiating work
- To consider your own practice.

SOME TRADITIONAL APPROACHES

Differentiation is the process whereby the levels of tasks set to students in class or for homework are matched to the known levels of performance and potential of the individual students involved.

These levels relate to topics we have discussed earlier in this book (pages 44–50): cognitive demand, and the requirement for students to progress in knowledge, understanding and skills.

In the commonest case scenario teachers make the pragmatic assumption that a class is roughly homogeneous in ability level; and they set a single task which makes the same demands on all the students: an undifferentiated task.

In practice, of course, students interpret the task differently because of their different ability levels; and thus the task becomes differentiated by outcome.

An example of this process would be something like this. The students are studying Tennyson's poem 'The Brook'. At an appropriate moment the teacher decides that the class should analyse what makes the poem effective. He sets an essay for homework: 'Explain what it is that makes Tennyson's poem "The Brook" such a lasting piece of work.' Some of the students produce fairly stock answers which reflect what has been said in class: the rhythm of the words, the pace of the language, the rural picture it paints, the repetition of ideas in new settings, and so on. But some students move the thinking on to look at the acute observation of the natural world, which appeals to a growing 'Green' faction in society; while others begin to talk about 'levels of meaning' in which the flow of the brook and the flow of life somehow interface.

This example shows what passes for differentiation in common parlance. But the point is that, strictly speaking, it is not. The task is not differentiated at all. It does produce a differentiated outcome, but that is not precisely the same thing.

It is difficult to be precise, but observation in classrooms suggests that differentiation by outcome, as a result of a single common task, happens on as many as 90 per cent of occasions when tasks are set.

This chapter and the next two challenge the adequacy of this pragmatic approach and put forward some ideas for alternative learning and teaching strategies to make differentiation more meaningful, and in particular they look at ways of building differentiation into tasks from the beginning as a *planned strategy*, not simply relying on outcomes.

Differentiation is a skill that is required of all teachers and one that has a profound effect on the quality of the learning provided by them. Hay McBer recognises this when it lists prominently in its definition of teaching skills the 'teacher behaviour' of 'using differentiation appropriately to challenge all pupils in the class' (para 1.2.1). This skill operates in a context of challenge and support for pupils to bring out the best learning in each individual, and that learning itself has to be set against a context of cognitive demand – something we discussed earlier in this book. Differentiation cannot, of course, work effectively unless the teacher is aware of the thinking levels of the work being pursued.

Differentiation, as we have seen, is about individual pupils: matching tasks to individuals' abilities and moving pupils on in the five domains identified in the first part of the book about learning objectives. This generalised view of the importance of differentiation is echoed in the White Paper (2001) para 3.15. In a context dealing with able children, teachers are urged to:

> *Blend increased pace, depth and breadth in varying proportions according to the ability and needs of pupils. We want teachers to consider express sets, fast tracking and more early entry to GCSE and advanced qualifications.*

One would expect this generalised advice to be made more specific in the Draft Handbook, and up to a point it is. Here are some of the things that are urged in that document.

> *Teachers must be able to:*
>
> *Where necessary, adapt class teaching objectives or identify specific teaching objectives for groups of pupils within the class or for individuals, in order to assist those pupils in reaching, surpassing, or coming as close as possible to reaching, the desired learning outcomes, challenging all pupils. (Draft Handbook para 3.1.1)*
>
> *(When dealing with bilingual pupils) analyse the demands of the teaching tasks to provide a suitable match, providing cognitive challenge as well as language support. (para 3.1.8)*
>
> *(With reference to the National Curriculum programmes of study) use grade descriptions to pitch activities and provide appropriate and challenging learning for all students in the class. (para 3.2.2)*
>
> *Enable all pupils, depending on their particular needs, to reach the targets for the class, or take appropriate steps towards reaching*

them, or exceed them. (para 3.2.5; cf. also 3.2.9 which deals with specific sub-groups such as those based on gender, culture, etc.)

These incidental mentions of differentiation are elucidated by a substantial paragraph (Draft Handbook 3.2.6) which it is worth quoting more fully. Before doing so, it might be worth repeating that differentiation is about meeting the needs of those pupils who have 'special educational needs' but also about meeting the needs of every individual pupil. The first section of the quoted paragraph deals with the latter, while the second spells out the implications for the former.

Those awarded Qualified Teacher Status (para 3.2.6) must demonstrate that they:

differentiate in their teaching to meet pupils' varying needs.

Examples

Those to be awarded QTS can differentiate to include and support all pupils through:

- monitoring individual responses in the course of teaching and creating opportunities for less confident pupils to participate;
- using discussion and questioning to provide challenges at a variety of levels according to the needs and levels of attainment of individuals and groups;
- encouraging peer support and co-operation;
- valuing responses and responding to misconceptions as they arise, in ways that help pupils understand and self-correct;
- recognising and building on individual success;
- being aware of and responsive to any individual's particular needs in accessing the curriculum through English;
- being aware of and responsive to any individual's particular needs in communication and interaction, cognition and learning, behavioural, emotional and social development, or physical and sensory development, and of the targets on pupils' IEPs;
- arranging opportunities for unfamiliar themes, concepts or required vocabulary or syntax to be taught or reinforced before a whole-class lesson to support individuals where necessary;
- providing bilingual support materials and/or additional visual materials where possible and appropriate;
- providing opportunities for pupils to talk through tasks within a supportive group or with an adult before being required to produce a piece of written work;
- providing structured 'writing frames' and extra materials to support reading and writing activities where necessary for groups or individuals;
- giving extra opportunities for consolidation and practice activities as necessary.

In relation to pupils with special educational needs, this includes:

- using a range of strategies to secure motivation and concentration;
- being aware of pupils' particular needs and of the targets in pupils' IEPs;
- providing examples to help pupils learn concepts; making explicit for them the links between one piece of learning and its generalisation to other settings;
- providing opportunities for practice and reinforcement of learning;
- making sure reading materials are suitable for pupils who find reading difficult;
- modifying tasks or using ICT to enable pupils who need help to communicate what they know and want to say in writing;
- using appropriate language and checking regularly for understanding;
- knowing how to develop pupils' understanding through the use of multi-sensory (visual, auditory and kinaesthetic) teaching approaches;
- knowing how and where to get advice from specialists on teaching styles and access strategies appropriate for pupils with less commonly occurring types of need – for example pupils with sensory or physical impairment, speech and language difficulties, autism or severe learning difficulties;
- with the advice and help of such specialists, organising learning opportunities and practical and physical activities so as to enable full participation in lessons.

The QTT document is less full compared with the Draft Handbook, but its advice (TTA 2002 paras 3.3.4 and 3.3.6) is similar. What is common to all of these official strictures and intentions is that, worthy as they are, they help practitioners very little, simply because there is no indication of *how* to achieve the desired ends. The aim of this third section of this book is to help practitioners to make differentiation work in classroom settings. As with the earlier material, all the examples quoted in what follows are real; and all the material incorporated in Tables and Activities has been tested in practice.

Activity 18

Reviewing your strategies for differentiation

Look back over all the tasks you have set in the last term. How many of them were common tasks set to a whole class/set/band?

How exactly did you differentiate for students of different abilities and stages of understanding?

What proportion of these tasks were differentiated other than by outcome?

Some common attempts at differentiation

Of course, most teachers are aware that differentiation in the way described is less than ideal. There are very real pressures – such as pressures of time and ease of marking – which make the ploy an attractive one. But it is possible to find some other approaches which attempt to overcome the problem of 'common' tasks.

Worksheets contain one of the more widespread approaches. Here, teachers often present a series of tasks, each a little more difficult than the previous one. In this way, everyone can complete a basic core of work which is covered by the earlier tasks; but some students can move on at their own pace (within the time-limits allocated) to more tricky work which makes more demands on their knowledge, skills and understanding.

Another form of differentiation that is quite common is to give specific tasks or additional support to the less able students in the class. Sometimes this method consists of quite sophisticated strategies – such as the use of a well-briefed ancillary – and at other times it simply means the teacher has to spend more time with the less able student while the others get on without help.

Sometimes it is suggested that ability grouping of one kind or another does away with the problem. This is a myth. Ability grouping can obviate the more extreme situations of overall spread of ability within the class; but it does not mean that all those within the streamed class will be performing at the same level or have the same needs. There is still a requirement for differentiation other than by outcome in order to match the task to the individual. A key word in differentiation is indeed the word 'individual'.

Another means to differentiation (rather than a method of differentiation) is the provision by the teacher of additional support materials. For example, a teacher may provide resources for slower learners which are easier to read. Or it may be that the most able are given additional material to cover so as to study the common class topic in more depth. This kind of support can aid the process of differentiation, though in itself it is not differentiation.

Sometimes, too, the teacher agrees with the class different outcomes for different students. He or she may agree that some students should present their work in written form (an essay, an exam-style answer) while others put their thoughts onto a tape-recorder or produce a working model. In the same way, teachers expect more from some students in a given period of time than from others. These are all manifestations of attempts at differentiation rather than methods for achieving it. Each has its uses, and individual methods of differentiation are discussed in more detail below.

Investigating differentiation in classrooms

Because of the difficulty of finding widespread good practice in differentiation it was decided both to research the literature on the subject, and to carry out some research at professional development days to ask a wide sample of teachers about their differentiation practice. This was done in a context of training about teaching strategies for the more able: since it is when dealing with extremes of ability that differentiation practice becomes more critical and teachers pay more attention to it.

(Likewise, reference to differentiation for the less able has been mentioned above.) What follows chronicles the outcomes of these processes.

Guidance on differentiation in the literature

The literature of able pupil education is full of exhortations to teachers to increase task demand and strengthen the cognitive content of classroom tasks (Vernon 1977, Wallace 1983, Freeman 1995). There is ample evidence to suggest that this is sound advice (Kerry 1984). For many teachers the reality of classroom life is that they teach in mixed ability contexts, in primary schools often in mixed age contexts as well. They are presented not only with task-setting for the 'core' group of pupils within the class – sometimes referred to as the middle band – but also a range of pupils of higher and lower ability, some of whom will be at relatively extreme ends of the intellectual continuum. Perhaps for this reason, advice to teachers about task demand has, in recent years, come to be grouped under the broader heading of differentiation. The teacher's skills of differentiation are, it is assumed, aimed more generally at pupils across the intellectual spectrum.

Differentiation rose to prominence on the education agenda after the 1988 Education Act. The ill-fated School Examinations and Assessment Council (SEAC, undated) produced a set of guidance books for teachers, one of which identified two methods of differentiation: by task and by outcome. This rather unsophisticated approach occupied just one page of their eighty-eight pages of guidance in the cited work.

Now that all classrooms are being inspected regularly by Ofsted inspectors, and that differentiation is high on their agenda when observing teaching skills, teachers are expected to show a range of skills in differentiating work for pupils. However, this fact epitomises the teacher's dilemma. For, while on the one hand Ofsted inspectors review teachers' differentiation skills when observing teaching, on the other hand the primary Handbook of Inspection (1995) does not contain the word in its index and does not refer explicitly to it in the text. Yet, inevitably, teachers have looked to official publications for guidance about how differentiation should work when well executed by a skilful practitioner. What advice has been available to them?

If Ofsted itself has been coy about setting down its criteria for effective differentiation, then some of its inspectors have been more forthcoming. Thus Laar (1995) in the *Times Educational Supplement* notes that a number of traditional approaches have been in common use:

- ordering the learning complexity of tasks set to pupils;
- devoting additional time to pupils with learning needs;
- grouping by ability;
- providing different (levels of) support material;
- accepting different levels of achievement and modes of presentation by pupils.

He goes on to suggest some additional strategies, notably that pupils in the same class can work on different 'strands' of the subject matter; that classroom assistants be used to support those who work with difficulty; that pupils should be encouraged to pursue personal interests within the subject in more depth.

HMI had some views on differentiation in the specific context of teaching the more able. In a review of practice (HMI, 1992) in primary and secondary schools they identified four methods of differentiation:

- by outcome;
- by rate of response;
- by enrichment;
- by setting different tasks.

But they warned that none of these worked unless they were built into the teacher's planning and used with a consciousness of desired outcome. For them, control was a keynote; and they were able to conclude:

> *The strategies were successful when the teacher had determined in advance what the pupil should learn, without excluding scope for originality. Consequently, the fourth strategy, in which differentiation had been built into the scheme of work and the planning of lessons, and in which explicit pathways to higher cognitive and intellectual development had been identified, was almost always associated with good practice.*
>
> (para 38)

This approach, while adding something beyond the SEAC contribution, has some inherent dangers in terms of the extent to which the pre-planning of the teacher (laudable in itself) could, in less competent hands, slip into over-control. Indeed, one such scenario is exemplified by Pollard (1994) in materials relating to the Open University's PGCE course. Pollard describes a primary class in which the social grouping and teaching strategies 'feed' the judgement of the teacher about differentiating work. What develops is the classic case of the self-fulfilling prophecy: in a context of high levels of pupil–pupil collaboration children on high-performing tables have access to more correct answers, and children on low-performing tables have less access – thus confirming the teachers' views of them as able and less able respectively. While tasks were differentiated, classroom organisation ensured that children could only continue to perform well or badly, and the desired outcomes of progress and improvement were negated.

To contrast with this, the government's favoured think-tank group on primary education produced a paper (Alexander, Rose and Woodhead, 1992) which claimed the exact opposite to be the desired outcome of differentiating classroom work:

> *Standards of education in primary schools will not rise until teachers expect more of their pupils, and, in particular, more of able and disadvantaged children.* (p. 32)

The remainder of their section on this topic is remarkably unhelpful and inexplicit, concluding:

> *... the best the teacher can do ... is to devise the classroom settings and pupil tasks which give the best chance of success.*   (p. 32)

Oddly enough, that is probably exactly what most teachers thought they were already trying to do; and they were looking to such prestigious publications to give them ideas and guidance: to no avail as it happened.

By far the most helpful document to come from an 'official' stable has been that from the National Council for Educational Technology (NCET). In this Dickson and Wright (1993) examine differentiation in some detail, showing that it can come through:

- content
- resource
- task
- outcome
- response
- support.

In a shortened version of this book (Open University, 1996) – designed for one of the most recent courses of initial teacher training and so, presumably, the repository of current wisdom and knowledge for the next generation of teachers – there is a significant discussion of how each of these methods of differentiation might work in practice, with examples from the classroom.

RESEARCHING TEACHERS' OWN METHODS OF DIFFERENTIATION

The consciousness of teachers for the need to differentiate across all classroom situations is due in no small measure to the emphasis placed on this range of strategies by various official pronouncements, as we have seen above. But our initial investigations seemed to suggest that little research had been undertaken either to explore systematically the feelings and collected professional wisdom of teachers about the recommended strategies, or to evaluate the effectiveness of the strategies with one of the key target groups of pupils at whom they are aimed: the more able. In this research we attempted an initial exploration of both of these matters.

We wanted to explore a number of issues:

- whether teachers use the recommended methods of differentiation;
- what happens when they do;
- the extent to which these recommended methods are deemed by teachers to be successful;
- how these methods relate specifically to the teaching of the more able pupils in primary and secondary classes.

With this agenda in mind we set out to gather information in two ways. Using opportunity samples of teachers in primary and secondary schools who were attending our in-service courses on teaching the more able, we devised two workshop tasks.

The first workshop task presented small groups of teachers with a list of the fifteen most regularly recommended methods of differentiation culled from the literature. Using a proforma (Figure 8.1), the teachers were asked to discuss and record two ways in which each of the fifteen methods proved successful in practice, and two ways in which they proved unsuccessful. In most cases the workshop members then produced a group response to the task. Over time we collected a number of these group responses from a variety of schools; we also collected some individual responses in situations where this was more appropriate.

In the second workshop task (Figure 8.2) we asked the staff:

- to articulate their desired outcomes from setting differentiated tasks to groups containing some able pupils;
- to describe a differentiated task they had set and to say why they thought it appropriate;
- to say what problems they had come across in setting differentiated tasks to more able pupils.

By using two different methods of gathering data we hoped to get a detailed and 'rounded' picture of the ways in which differentiation worked, or did not work, and some insight into the reasons. We wanted to move from the theoretical models to some practical experience which could be built into advice for teachers.

Workshop Task 1 proved to be an engaging task which teachers enjoyed: they found the discussion which it triggered enlightening – in secondary schools this was especially so when carried out in cross-departmental groups. The outcomes were interesting in that what we gained was a substantial insight into the advantages and disadvantages of the fifteen recommended methods of differentiation. These are discussed in some detail in Chapter 9 of this book. But this is an appropriate moment at which to try the task for yourself.

Activity 19

Assessing methods of differentiation

Use the proforma from Figure 8.1 to assess your own views of fifteen common methods of differentiation identified by other teachers.

Consider each of the fifteen methods in turn, and write down two advantages and two disadvantages for it.

When you have done this, keep your completed proforma, and compare it with the results which you will find in Chapter 9.

What do we want to achieve through differentiation?

Workshop Task 2, referred to above, probed the intentions behind differentiation. In the first three chapters of this book there was an

Figure 8.1

Methods of differentiation: a proforma

Method of differentiation	Pros	Cons
Using graduated worksheets		
Making available resource packs of additional information		
Asking open questions more often		
Using individual pupil contracts/targets		
Challenging pupils' assumptions and received values		
Increasing the use of support teachers or parent helpers		
Encouraging self-pacing by pupils		
Removing unnecessary repetition (e.g. multiple similar examples to be worked)		
Using homework time for the production of an extended project		
Promoting self-marking/self-criticism by pupils of their work		
Allowing pupils to record responses in different ways, e.g. pictures, cartoons, audiotapes, graphs		
Asking cognitively demanding questions		
Setting tasks with no single correct solution		
Using role play		
Setting tasks with increased thinking demand		

analysis of learning intentions: and in using various methods of differentiation it was possible to extend the learning intentions of lessons.

The outcomes from this second task can be seen in Table 8.1 on page 92.

DRAWING TOGETHER THE THEMES OF THIS CHAPTER

Differentiation is an important, planned aspect of effective task-setting. It is the way in which tasks can be consciously matched to the individual

Figure 8.2

Proforma for collecting teachers' views

Differentiating classroom tasks for able pupils

One of the commonest strategies for dealing with able pupils in the classroom is to set them a task which is differentiated from the tasks set to other pupils.

In this activity we are interested in the criteria for differentiation which teachers use and in the processes of setting differentiated tasks to the more able.

Please write a freehand response to each of the following questions.

1 When you set a separate differentiated task to more able pupils, what are the outcomes you hope to achieve by doing this? e.g. 'buying some time until other pupils catch up'.

   a . . . .

   b . . . .

   c . . . .

   d . . . .

2 Please describe briefly a differentiated task you have set to more able pupils and then say why you thought it was appropriate.

   a Task: . . . .

   b Why appropriate: . . . .

     . . . .

     . . . .

3 What problems do you come across in trying to differentiate tasks or in using a range of differentiated tasks with able pupils in the classroom?

   a . . . .

   b . . . .

   c . . . .

---

needs and abilities of students. This in turn enhances the effectiveness of the teacher's learning objectives for lessons. Well differentiated tasks keep students more interested in their work, and lay the foundation for improved progress. Differentiation may indeed be a means of helping to assess and measure progress in learning. The commonest form of differentiation – differentiation by outcome – is, arguably, not a genuine method of differentiation at all since it is not 'built in' but is an 'incidental'.

There is too little 'official' guidance about what constitutes effective differentiation, though professional wisdom can throw some light on a wide range of strategies. In the next chapter we take a more detailed look at the fifteen strategies (listed in Figure 8.1 above), and at what teachers have to say about them.

Table 8.1

Teachers' desired outcomes from differentiated tasks

1   To increase pupils' knowledge/understanding of a particular area of study.
2   To enable pupils to engage in their own research.
3   To increase pupils' skills in self-research/working on their own.
4   To try to get more able pupils to ask questions, e.g. 'Why things happen' and 'What are the facts?'
5   To create a greater need to want to understand our world.
6   To develop confidence and self-reliance.
7   To encourage questioning and problem solving.
8   To challenge the pupils and stretch the more able.
9   To match the task to the able pupil's higher ability.
10 To extend the able pupil's thinking beyond their usual level.
11 To offer pupils the opportunity of a challenge.
12 To widen their knowledge and skills both in breadth and depth of knowledge.
13 To buy time.
14 To produce display work.
15 To complete research which may be passed on to others.
16 To sustain the interest of the pupil.
17 To use the able pupil's time effectively.
18 To prevent boredom setting in.
19 To make the work more satisfying for the pupil involved.
20 To set challenges and push boundaries.
21 To see just how far pupils can be pushed!
22 To develop higher order skills.
23 To allow the able pupil to go into more detail.
24 To allow the able pupil to use vocabulary that is relevant to the task.
25 To allow the able pupil to use or illustrate some recent example of grammar that has been covered in a whole class lesson.
26 To give pupils a chance to express themselves more fully.
27 To give pupils extra knowledge of the subject.
28 To enable pupils to become more self-critical.

Outcomes

At the end of this chapter you should have:

● Reflected at length about the range of practice in differentiating work and compared your own practice with this
● Understood how differentiation relates to the previous topics of the book: formulating learning objectives and task-setting
● Made some judgements about the advantages and disadvantages of different methods of differentiation.

REFERENCES

Alexander, R., Rose, J. and Woodhead, C. (1992) *Curriculum Organisation and Classroom Practice in Primary Schools*. London: DES

Dickinson, C. and Wright, J. (1993) *Differentiation: a practical handbook of classroom strategies*. Coventry: NCET

Freeman, J., Span, P. and Wagner, J. (1995) *Actualising Talent*. London: Cassell

HMI (1992) *Education observed: the education of very able children in maintained schools*. London: DES

Kerry, T. (1984) 'Analysing the cognitive demand made by classroom tasks in mixed ability classes' in Wragg, E.C. (1984) *Classroom Teaching Skills*. London: Croom Helm

Laar, B. (1995) 'An inspector writes' *Times Educational Supplement*, 8.12.95

Ofsted (1995) *The Ofsted Handbook: Guidance on the Inspection of Nursery and Primary Schools*. London: HMSO

Open University (1996) *Extracts from NCET: Differentiation*. Milton Keynes: Open University Press

Pollard, A. (1994) 'Coping strategies and the multiplication of differentiation in infant classrooms' in Bourne, J. (1994) *Thinking Through Primary Practice*. London: OU/Routledge.

SEAC (undated) *A Guide to Teacher Assessment Pack C: A sourcebook for teacher assessment*. London: Heinemann

Vernon, P., Adamson, G. and Vernon, D. (1977) *The Psychology and Education of Gifted Children*. London: Methuen

Wallace, B. (1983) *Teaching Very Able Children*. London: Ward Lock

9

DIFFERENTIATION IN PRACTICE: THE TEACHERS'
PERSPECTIVES

OBJECTIVES

This chapter invites you:

- To consider other teachers' views of how differentiation methods work
- To evaluate a variety of approaches of differentiation.

AN OVERVIEW OF THE RESEARCH ON METHODS OF DIFFERENTIATION

In the previous chapter it was indicated that, as part of our research into differentiation, we asked a large sample of teachers to reflect on fifteen common methods of differentiation. These were listed in Figure 8.1. The outcome of this process was that, over time and across a variety of primary and secondary schools, we were able to gain a good feel for the ways in which teachers found these different methods usable and useful. We were able, too, to track what the drawbacks to each method were. In contrast to the literature on the subject, the professional wisdom about differentiation was able to pinpoint both the good and the bad features within each method (that is, rather than merely comparing and contrasting one method with another). At the risk of labouring this point it is our intention to set out here the pros and cons of each of the methods investigated, as reported to us by our teacher respondents. In each case we have included only the most frequently reported advantages and disadvantages. This is done most economically in a series of Tables (Tables 9.1 to 9.15) below.

Before you go on to study the Tables that follow, read and bear in mind Activity 20. When you have studied the Tables 9.1 to 9.15 revisit Activity 20 and complete it.

Activity 20

Assessing the value of different methods of differentiation
Tables 9.1 to 9.15 set out the pros and cons, the strengths and weaknesses, of fifteen methods of differentiation, as teachers in our sample saw them.
Implicit in this analysis is a strategy for how each method can be most appropriately used.
As you read each Table try to answer these questions for each method:

- How would I use this method?
- For what purpose?

- For which groups of students?
- When would I avoid this method?
- How can this method contribute to a balanced programme of differentiation, to provide variety in my lessons?

Pros
- provides plenty of work for pupils to do
- uses appropriate language
- good for reinforcement
- stretches children
- pupils can work at their own pace
- provides self-pacing

Cons
- able pupils can avoid challenging work
- may have restricted outcomes
- is an invidious way of indicating level of work
- may not target gifted pupils accurately
- may require teacher's support if not understood
- limited teacher/pupil interaction results

Table 9.1

Method 1: Using graduated worksheets

Pros
- encourages children to work with large quantities of data
- is useful for extension work
- develops further knowledge
- may provide extra stimulation/interest
- may provide more demanding material
- may provide more open-ended tasks

Cons
- makes extra preparation work for the teacher
- is time-consuming
- is costly
- can be more of the same
- may inhibit the less able
- resources may date rapidly

Table 9.2

Method 2: Making available resource packs of additional information

Pros
- allows scope for creativity
- encourages pupil to think more
- engages pupil's attention
- is challenging and builds rapport
- is not time-consuming for the teacher

Cons
- is hard for teacher to do successfully
- needs preparation
- may produce peer group derision
- is less good for quieter pupils
- could take wrong route
- may be intimidating (especially to those of lower ability)

Table 9.3

Method 3: Asking open questions more often

Pros
- increases motivation
- leads to precise learning
- gives pupil ownership of learning
- sees pupil as an individual
- gives pupil clear goals
- creates challenge

Cons
- is time-consuming for the teacher
- is a paperwork nightmare
- needs constant monitoring
- needs good record-keeping
- targets may have to be changed
- targets may be aimed too low/high

Table 9.4

Method 4: Using individual contracts/targets

Pros
- makes pupil think deeply
- moves pupil on and encourages independent thought
- develops pupils' own values
- challenges complacency
- encourages creativity
- sets tasks appropriately

Cons
- can undermine parents' values
- causes pupils to feel intimidated
- could be confrontational
- can knock pupils' confidence
- could result in alienation
- may result in criticism being construed negatively

Table 9.5

Method 5: Challenging pupils' assumptions and received values

Table 9.6

Method 6: Increasing the use of support teachers or parent helpers

Pros
- encourages the child
- increases motivation and enthusiasm
- gives more adult support
- broadens parents' understanding
- can help meet individual needs and can only serve to help them
- releases main class for teacher

Cons
- is expensive
- may have training implications
- some pupils don't like individual support
- some pupils become dependent upon individual support
- adult may not be sufficiently skilled
- parents may have set ideas

Table 9.7

Method 7: Encouraging self-pacing by pupils

Pros
- is an efficient use of time
- makes pupils independent
- helps pupils learn how to learn
- takes pressure off teacher
- develops expectations of self
- teaches time-management skills

Cons
- can be abused
- needs a lot of monitoring
- might be their weak area
- encourages some pupils to 'slack'
- allows pupils to move on without knowledge/ understanding/skills
- gives scope to those underachieving because of lack of effort

Table 9.8

Method 8: Removing unnecessary repetition (e.g. multiple similar exercises to be worked)

Pros
- saves time to be spent on harder tasks
- stops boredom
- allows pupils to increase their knowledge of other topics
- leaves more time for progress
- removes disruption
- sustains motivation

Cons
- removes chance of revision and consolidation
- means teacher has to prepare extra work
- results in boredom
- denies opportunities for reinforcement

Table 9.9

Method 9: Using homework time for an extended project

Pros
- is motivational
- encourages initiative
- uses home/town library resources
- is self-pacing
- allows for creativity
- improves study skills

Cons
- is hard because of lack of books in disadvan- taged homes
- leads to pupil burn-out
- is open to abuse
- needs to be shaped by teacher
- can be repetitive
- may mean student feels 'left to it'

Table 9.10

Method 10: Promoting self-marking/ self-criticism by pupils of their work

Pros
- demonstrates deeper levels of thought
- focuses attention
- promotes responsibility
- allows for analysis of own skills
- develops evaluative skills and recognition of standards
- teaches about targets

Cons
- is easier for objective tasks
- requires a good mark scheme
- is open to abuse, cheating
- doesn't relieve teacher of need to see work
- may falter because pupils tend to underes- timate their own standard
- may miss out some relevant criteria

Pros

- gives scope for different talents
- is quicker
- provides novelty value
- gives freedom of expression
- develops knowledge of working with a variety of media
- encourages self-motivation

Cons

- encourages avoidance techniques
- falls foul of expense of resources
- means that teacher may need to develop new skills
- means pupils may have to develop the necessary skills
- is time-consuming
- is difficult to mark

Table 9.11

Method 11: Allowing pupils to record responses in different ways, e.g. pictures, cartoons, audio tape, graphs

Pros

- reinforces knowledge
- reaches those who need targeting
- develops pupils' own understanding
- stretches pupils
- helps reasoning skills
- shows there are no clear answers

Cons

- makes it difficult for the pupil to work alongside less able friends
- may make some pupils feel threatened
- is time-consuming
- may demotivate less able
- may pressurise the more able
- requires increased preparation of demanding questions by teacher

Table 9.12

Method 12: Asking cognitively demanding questions

Pros

- is realistic, teaches about life
- encourages creativity
- encourages self-motivation
- means pupils are forced to substantiate claims
- means pupils can achieve their own standards and work to improve upon them
- can provide creative, thoughtful outcomes

Cons

- may be depressing
- is perhaps available only to part of the class
- becomes meaningless?
- can provide a sense of existential despair
- needs more resources
- makes more work for teachers

Table 9.13

Method 13: Setting tasks with no single correct solution

Pros

- encourages empathetic thinking
- encourages social interaction
- allows learning to take place in a more relaxed atmosphere
- takes pupil beyond the normal range of responses
- leads to holistic learning
- gives opportunities for different interpretation

Cons

- means shy, nervous pupils hide
- can be mechanical
- is time-consuming to set up properly
- threatens some pupils
- produces problems of control
- is too difficult a concept for some pupils

Table 9.14

Method 14: Using role play

Pros

- means bright children are often intrigued by the challenge
- stimulates
- stretches those who can think for themselves and be creative
- promotes problem solving and extension
- motivates

Cons

- causes problems with assessment
- requires tasks to be structured
- can be demotivating for less able
- inhibits those who need guidance
- may promote daydreaming
- means increased preparation for teacher
- demands teacher skills
- means lack of understanding by pupil may 'turn them off'

Table 9.15

Method 15: Setting tasks with increased thinking demand

We believe that the findings from this research are unique in two important ways. They demonstrate an insight into the thinking of teachers themselves, which is lacking in most of the literature; and they demonstrate a subtlety of approach to each method of differentiation which is certainly not a feature of official publications and pronouncements. To illustrate this we can return to our four research questions, outlined earlier on pages 88–89.

Do teachers use the 'recommended' methods of differentiation?

The answer is yes: but they use them with caution, and not uncritically. Teachers do not find them to be blanket solutions to the problems of matching in the classroom, and they are certainly not always successful, even with more able pupils. For each method quoted the 'cons' are finely balanced with the 'pros' – and there is an emphasis on the need to take contextual factors into account when deciding whether the method is appropriate. A good example of this is in the use of Method 1: Using graduated worksheets (Table 9.1). The positive view is that this method is effective if used sparingly, to aid students' self-pacing and to bring about a match of task to student; indeed it may help class management and it has the advantage that it gives teachers confidence precisely because it is a 'recommended' method. But the negative aspects of this method are considerable: it does not guarantee a 'match' between task and pupil and may even miss the opportunity of challenge for the more able. There is a danger of boredom ('death by worksheet'). For the teacher there is a resource implication relating to extra preparation time and also monitoring of a different set of student work. Some students may find the process divisive in highlighting their ability and alienating them from peers. Thus, even when the fundamental 'recommended' aim of matching is achieved, the overall educational value of this method may, in certain contexts, be somewhat wide of the mark.

What happens when teachers use the 'recommended' methods of differentiation?

As we have seen, teachers do use recommended methods of differentiation even though they treat them with a degree of scepticism. This process has been described above in relation to the first method in Table 9.1: using graduated worksheets. The same picture emerges for the remaining fourteen methods listed there.

Thus we see that the use of additional resources is seen by teachers to be useful because it extends the scope of any given topic, especially for the more able, providing increased task demand, improved opportunity for open-ended study and a close match with reading ability. The drawbacks are in terms of production time for the teacher, limitations of cost, and the danger of the work becoming mere extension rather than enrichment. In the same way, asking more open-ended questions would appear to be a logical differentiation strategy for use in classes of mixed ability or those containing able students; and it is. Such a ploy can encourage creativity and promote lateral thinking; all students will be challenged and may improve their skills of articulation of knowledge. But the downside is that it requires considerable skill from the teacher, it may disadvantage slower learners, and even some more able pupils may find the process of challenge daunting.

Learning contracts, too, have their pros and cons. The individualisation of work can be a gain; and so can the potential for pacing the work of youngsters more appropriately. Yet formal contracts represent administrative labour and the tracking of progress can be time-consuming; some students don't like their levels of ability to be identified in this way, either. Similarly, just as asking open-ended questions is challenging, so the challenging of students' assumptions may be viewed negatively by parents or be seen by students themselves as threatening; and this despite the best intentions of encouraging deeper thought and more extended reasoning skills.

Some of the recommended methods are, in practical terms, more under the control of the teacher than others. Using support staff and parents may prove valuable in allowing real needs to be targeted and in terms of student encouragement; but the problem in many schools is that such help can be expensive and often does not exist. Even where it does exist it requires careful management. So can self-pacing by more able students – apparently undemanding of resource – be used effectively? Yes, it can: it provides the student with a greater ownership of learning, with time-management skills and with motivation, possibly. But even here teachers are aware that the more idle can fail to benefit from this option and underachievement may actually be encouraged.

Even with a method of differentiation as simple as removing the unnecessary repetition of multiple examples (e.g. of maths problems relating to a topic the student has already understood) there is dispute about the efficacy. While this can be seen as a way of gaining time for more worthwhile activities, some teachers favour the multiple examples as a means of revision and reinforcement. But if opinion is divided on this, homework is even more contentious as a means of differentiating work by setting extended projects from which more able pupils may have opportunities to benefit. For some able youngsters this may be seen as an opportunity for extension, providing motivation and an outlet for interest, as well as a chance to gain extra knowledge against an assessment target. But many able students simply resent being expected to do more work than their peers; they may not have adequate support and resources at home to allow proper benefit to accrue, or may be oversupported or pushed too hard by ambitious parents.

While teachers are very much aware of the time pressures on them and might be expected to favour students' self-marking and self-criticism as one means of tackling the marking chore, they are aware of drawbacks. For some students, it might represent a real chance to become analytical and independent, but for others it is a chance to cheat, to over-assess or under-play their skills. But if self-marking is ambiguous as a means to differentiate work, even for the more able, then allowing students to record their responses to classroom tasks in various media is even more problematic. This method depends on stretched resources, requires specific skills in students which they may not have, and provides the teacher with increased problems of assessment for work on the same topic in varying formats. So the values – motivation through variety, student-centredness, freedom of expression, for example – can be outweighed in some circumstances.

Asking cognitively demanding questions is a commonly recommended method of differentiating classroom work for the more able and – for all students – may help reasoning skills, contribute an element of curiosity and demonstrate that to some questions there are no clear answers. But in a mixed ability group the process can be divisive: and even the able may be demoralised if the teacher fails to pitch the demand accurately. In the same way, setting tasks with no single correct solution, or tasks with increased thinking demand, can be a double-edged sword for all the same reasons.

Finally, a common suggestion is to use role play: this may give opportunities for more affective responses to knowledge, providing useful life-skills. Its value is limited, though, in that many students are too shy and vulnerable to respond, and the class management implications may stretch the teacher's own skills.

To what extent are the 'recommended' methods of differentiation deemed by teachers to be successful?

The brief review of teachers' assessments of various methods of differentiation (above) has again stressed that each method must be separately reviewed and weighed for both its strength and weakness within the teaching context in which it is selected. This is the fundamental and recurrent insight of this research, and the feature which marks it out from most of the 'official' guidance on methods of differentiation.

How do the 'recommended' methods of differentiation relate specifically to the teaching of more able students in primary and secondary schools?

To answer this question it is appropriate to turn back to the data summarised in Table 8.1 in Chapter 8 (page 92). Table 8.1 told us what teachers hoped to achieve through differentiation for able pupils. The salient points were as follows.

Differentiation is about individual challenge: increasing knowledge, skills and understanding. This involves getting students to ask themselves the all-important 'why?' questions, and to solve problems. Differentiation is also about using time effectively: eliminating boredom, pushing back the boundaries of knowledge, capturing interest, practising language skills. Part of that process is the inculcation of study skills and, alongside that, to give a self-critical confidence and sure-footedness to learning.

SUMMARY

Differentiation was the watchword of the 1990s, and has now taken its place among the key criteria for effective classroom practice. Yet much of the advice on this subject has originated in official publications which have, it is suggested, lacked the critical edge of practitioner expertise. In our research we found both primary and secondary teachers struggling to carry out the 'recommendations' of official pronouncements; their strategies have embraced all the main methods of differentiation: of content, resource, task, outcome, response and support. But the practitioners have found that there are subtleties of procedures and strategy which have not been, to date, catered for in the literature. This chapter has attempted to reveal some of these.

Outcomes

At the end of this chapter you should have:

- Reflected at length on a variety of different techniques for differentiating work for your own pupils
- Made judgements about what might work or not work in your situation, and identified additional techniques to try out
- Recognised the need to relate the techniques for differentiation that you choose to the desired outcomes for the work of pupils
- Developed a more critical approach to using differentiation techniques in your own classroom.

---

10 HOW DIFFERENTIATION HELPS

OBJECTIVES

This chapter invites you:

- To follow the process of differentiation through a sequence of lessons taken from a real classroom
- To make connections between the requirements of the National Standards, the previous material in this manual, and the process of teaching in a differentiated way.

INTRODUCTION

In this last chapter of the trio on differentiation we move on to look at how differentiation can be used to maximise the learning of students in the classroom. To do this I have taken an example from Key Stage 2, from the science curriculum, and from the section on Living Things. But first it is important to have some background about the students and the task.

The material in this chapter is material that has been used with pupils in actual classrooms and for demonstration lessons. The material conforms with the requirements both of the National Curriculum (for context) and the TTA documents (2001, 2002).

BACKGROUND

The set of differentiated tasks described below formed part of the outcome of a study of living things with a year-group of about 65 Year 6 students in a suburban primary school. The students were housed in a large open-plan teaching area, which was well furnished but rather short on facilities (the area had been newly built and was not yet fully equipped). Organisation was mixed ability; a number of students had mild learning difficulties, one was statemented; but at the other extreme of the ability range there were several very able students. The two teachers worked either separately or together, according to need; and there was an ancillary who helped the statemented student. On this occasion, one teacher provided the lead for a series of lessons spread over one week and totalling about six hours of classroom time on the theme of Living Things. She chose to start the work using Owls as the stimulus.

(Those who would like to do so may wish to pursue the content of part of this lesson sequence which is used in the companion book in this series: *Explaining and Questioning*. However, it is not essential to an understanding of the point made here to pursue this cross-reference. The learning objectives for this lesson sequence are discussed in Chapter 1 of this book.)

The short sequence of lessons was planned to take account of the points made earlier in this book about formulating effective learning objectives. Figure 10.1, therefore, sets out the planning for the sequence using a proforma very similar to the one described earlier in Figure 2.1 (page 22).

OVERALL SESSION PLAN (4 lessons)

CURRICULUM AREA: Science Key Stage 2 Year 6
Life Processes and Living Things
Living things in their environment

INTENTIONS:

- To introduce and give insight into some key concepts: adaptation, habitat, territory, eco-system
- To link the work with previous learning, e.g. food webs and food chains
- To give a context to the work within scientific processes: observing, hypothesising, using data and evidence, drawing conclusions
- To link scientific and aesthetic responses.

RELATION TO KEY STAGE 2 NC:

The work will be centred in Section 5 – Living things and their environment. The students have been on a visit to a nature trail which illustrated 5a, 5b. The knowledge will be extended to 5c, 5d. This will be achieved by using and reinforcing processes in Investigative Science, i.e. 1c, d, e, 2b and 3a, b, c. The students will look at the interactions between owls and hedgerows to examine scientific concepts. They will work across subject boundaries into art and English, with an aesthetic appreciation of the objects of study (see National Curriculum English KS2 Writing 2a, b; Speaking and listening 1a; and art 7a, b).

CONTENT LESSON BY LESSON – OUTLINE:

1 Observation, deduction – concept of adaptation – these reinforced using pre-prepared worksheets
2 Habitat (including different kinds of adaptation); ideas of territory and the eco-system. Digestion in owls – experiments, hypotheses, evidence and conclusions
3 Aesthetic responses: science and the arts. Owl poems. Start of graded tasks
4 Compiling of draft work into finished products for 'Our book of Owls'.

Intended outcomes:

- A record of personal learning
- A class book about owls.

DIFFERENTIATION:

To be achieved mainly through a series of differentiated tasks targeted at specific students' needs and levels of ability.

Figure 10.1

Planning for a sequence of lessons on Living Things – Owls

KEY RESOURCES:

Stuffed owl; specially prepared worksheets on adaptation; owl proforma for sketching resource materials for each of the tasks to be set; task cards.

TEACHING AND LEARNING METHODS:

Whole class work for initial information and stimulus.
Individual work for recording.
Individualised and group work for carrying out tasks.

CURRICULUM LINKS:

Varied from one student to another, but including links with art, poetry, literature, and mathematics.

PLANNED ASSESSMENT STRATEGIES:

Feedback through question and answer including higher order questions.
Shared, differentiated tasks.
Final contributions to 'Our book of Owls' by individuals.

EVALUATION:

(To be completed after the sessions.)

DIAGRAM OF LESSON CONTENT

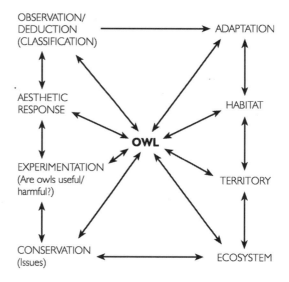

LESSON I

Lesson objectives (knowledge, skills, understanding, attitudinal, affective)

At the end of this session the students will be able to:

1 Observe acutely and articulate the value of observation
2 Deduce intelligently and articulate the value of deduction
3 Understand the concept of adaptation
4 Draw conclusions based on evidence
5 Enjoy looking at the stuffed owl, and at the scientific processes

Outlines of content and sequence

Solve owl riddle
Observe specimen
See: characteristics of its eyes, ears, bill, legs, feet, claws, feathering
Deduce: kills for a living – how? when? where? what?

Creature does not exist in isolation – ADAPTED to its surroundings

Definition

Relationship with other learning

Link with nature trail visit. Drawing from life.

Materials and resources

Stuffed owl. Owl pictures (various media). Riddle cards. Worksheets.

Teaching and learning methods

Whole class stimulus. Questioning to draw out skills, understanding.

Tasks to be set / methods of differentiation

Drawing from life. Using drawing to illustrate adaptation.

Student assessment

To be achieved through questioning and responses to tasks set.

Lesson evaluation

(To be completed after the lesson.)

LESSON 2

Lesson objectives (knowledge, skills, understanding, attitudinal, affective)
At the end of this session the students will be able to:
1   Understand and define habitat
2   Understand additional kinds of adaptation
3   Explain ecosystem
4   React to owls and other creatures in a variety of ways – scientific and aesthetic

Outlines of content and sequence

Recap lesson 1. Observe: hedgerow – height – long, narrow corridor, effect of this on habitat size, variety of shrubs etc. involved, undergrowth, variety of other wildlife involved.

Deduce: varied food supply. How plentiful? What factors affect this?
Vulnerability – human disturbance, farming methods. Type of area used.
Territory/habitat – differences. Link territory, habitat, food chains.

Relationship with other learning

See lesson 1.

Materials and resources

Hedgerow mock-up. Worksheet – what scientists do.

Teaching and learning methods

Whole class – shared data. Question and answer; didactic – but aimed at higher order thinking.

Tasks to be set / methods of differentiation

Worksheet for reinforcement.

Student assessment

Through feedback.

Lesson evaluation

(To be completed after the lesson.)

LESSON 3

Lesson objectives (knowledge, skills, understanding, attitudinal, affective)

At the end of this session the students will be able to:

1 Recall concepts: habitat, territory, adaptation
2 Explain how scientists observe, guess, test, draw conclusions
3 Apply the foregoing to understanding owl digestion
4 Understand how to gather and use data about owl feeding
5 Link knowledge of owls to examples of owl poetry, literature.

Outlines of content and sequence

Explain owl digestive system and reasons for it
Pellets
Identification charts for pellet contents
Some exploded pellets
Worksheet for data recording explained
Equipment for dissection of pellets
Two owl poems

Relationship with other learning

See previous plans.

Materials and resources

Pellets
Examples of dissected pellets
Dissecting equipment
Hygiene equipment
Worksheets; texts of poems to be read

Teaching and learning methods

Some didactic introduction. Question and answer. Hands-on experimental work. Recording findings. Listening carefully to poetry.

Tasks to be set / methods of differentiation

Students will have the chance to dissect a pellet, and to try writing some owl poetry. In any leftover time they will begin the graded tasks – individually or in assigned groups – that will lead to 'Our book of Owls'. Differentiation in the last will be through careful assignment of students to cognitively graded tasks, with options to move on when they have achieved their own first goals.

Student assessment

By quality of outcome.

Lesson evaluation

(To be completed after the lesson.)

LESSON 4

Lesson objectives (knowledge, skills, understanding, attitudinal, affective)

At the end of this session the students will be able to:

1 Contribute an entry to 'Our book of Owls'
2 Apply all the scientific concepts for the course by applying it to the set task
3 Complete one task well at their own level, and maybe move on
4 Have enjoyed the sessions on owls and scientists
5 Work collaboratively to achieve a shared goal.

Outlines of content and sequence

Personal work on graded tasks (shown below).

Relationship with other learning

Continued inter-disciplinary approach, with art, literature and mathematics included in the theme.

Materials and resources

Task cards. Equipment related to each task card. Class resource collection to aid personal work.

Teaching and learning methods

Mainly group work, though some individuals may complete some work individually.
Collaborative product for the shared outcome – the owl book.

Tasks to be set / methods of differentiation

Tasks graded as shown; students allocated to appropriate task groups.

Student assessment

Through task outcomes.

Lesson evaluation

(To be completed after the lesson.)

A brief comment on lesson content

The outline content of the lessons is shown in Figure 10.1, and for the present purpose there is little need to elaborate on the information provided. What was important for the teacher was to determine effective lesson outcomes. She needed to discover the extent of student learning, to monitor what had and had not been learned effectively (feedback), to set meaningful tasks to this end, and to match the tasks – as far as possible in a large class group – to individual need. All of these intentions are in line with what has been discussed in Chapters 4 to 7 earlier in this book.

Setting differentiated tasks

To this end the teacher decided to set a series of differentiated tasks. She was aware that she needed to set some tasks for the less able, and some for the more able, and that she needed to have a variety of tasks which would extend the learning of specific students in specific directions. These judgements came out of her knowledge of the student group as individuals. She therefore set about devising a range of tasks. However, she felt strongly that a class theme like this should have a flavour of co-operative enterprise about it. In other words, she wanted all the students to feel that they had actually contributed to a shared outcome which could bind the work together for everyone, in addition to completing their individual portions of work. For this reason she planned that all the task outcomes should be filed in a special folder entitled 'Our book of Owls' which could be put into the class library and shared with other classes as appropriate.

Given these overall intentions, the class teacher set about devising the series of tasks which would be shared among the students. The following paragraphs describe those tasks in as much detail as is necessary to give the tenor of them.

Owl level 1

DESIGN A COVER

Design a cover for a book about owls.
Make the main feature of your cover an imaginative picture of an owl – the pictures on this card are meant to start you thinking.
Come up with some ideas of your own!
Include the title in the cover design:

Our book of Owls

Your cover should be A4 size, this way up →
Make your cover on a sheet of card OR mount it on card when it is finished.

Owl level 2

OWL FOOD CHAIN

The owl is a predator and so it is at the top of its food chain. Make a neat diagram of a Little Owl's food chain.

- Do this on plain A4 paper and use a line guide when you write.
- Put a heading: FOOD CHAIN OF A LITTLE OWL.
- Draw the food chain carefully.
- Label all the creatures and plants you draw.
- IF YOU HAVE TIME ... Colour the finished diagram with PALE colours, e.g. watercolour wash.

Owl level 3

OWL CARTOON

Imagine you are the editor of a magazine about birds.
You want to explain to young children how owls live.
You decide to do it by using a series of cartoon pictures and
captions (look at the example).

- Draw and caption a series of cartoons explaining how an owl
  lives.

Owl level 4

OWL POEMS

Look at the printed sheets. Read the poem called TOWN OWL and
the one called DISTURBANCES.
Think about what these poems mean.

- On a sheet of lined paper put the title: Owl Poems.
- Now say which of the poems you liked best.
- Now go on and explain why you made this choice.

(When you are writing say which words or sentences in the poem
you liked or did not like; say whether the poets do or don't like
owls; tell us which bits of the poems you liked most.)

Owl level 5

OWLS AND HEDGEROWS

Owls depend on hedgerows.
1 On a piece of plain A4 paper (this way up → ⬚) draw a
  diagram (sketch) of a hedgerow like the one below. Put in all the
  things you can think of that grow in a hedgerow.
2 Label all the things you have drawn, like this:
  - oak   - tree layer
  - hawthorn   - hedge layer
  - grass   - undergrowth
3 On the diagram labelled 'Improving the habitat for owls' carry
  out these tasks:
  - The diagram shows a big field. How could the farmer divide
    the field into four to make the best habitat for owls? (Draw
    your answer on the sheet.)
  - Answer the questions on the bottom of the sheet.

i) In what other ways could the farmer make his field attractive to
   owls (for example, how could he encourage an owl to nest?)
ii) Why might a farmer find it useful to have an owl around the
   farm?

Owl level 6

KINDS OF OWL IN BRITAIN

1 How many kinds of owl can be seen in the British Isles? (Use the CDs/books to find the information.)

2 (On A4 lined paper) Make a neat list of the kinds of owls you discover.

3 Each of these kinds of owl lives in a slightly different kind of habitat and eats slightly different food. Make a table like the one below to show the type of owl, its habitat and its food:

Type of owl	Habitat	Food
Little owl		
Barn owl		
(and so on)		

4 By looking at the books, can you work out ways in which each kind of owl has adapted differently from the others? (Here is a clue: think about things like size, colour, shape . . .)

Write your answers below the table you have drawn.

Owl level 7

OWL PELLETS

Ask the teacher for some contents from an owl's pellet and an identification chart.

Try to identify what creatures the owl has eaten. Make a list of the creatures you identify.

Write this list on a sheet of A4 lined paper:

- Put the heading: CONTENTS OF AN OWL'S PELLET.
- Make a list.
- Write a few lines about your findings (for example: were the remains hard to identify; did you find anything that surprised you? and so on).

Owl level 8

OWL EATING

On the sheets there is information about food taken by a Tawny Owl

- in the country
- in the rural outskirts of London
- in Holland Park (a city area).

1 Write two or three paragraphs setting down the differences in the owl's feeding habits between the three places.

2 In each case, give some reasons why you think these owls were feeding like this in the three different habitats.

Owl level 9

COMPARING OWLS

On the sheets you will find information about:

- the food taken by a Tawny Owl living in a woodland habitat, and
- the food taken by a Barn Owl living in a farmland habitat.

Look at this carefully and then answer these questions (write the answers on A4 lined paper).

1 How many reasons can you think of to explain the differences between the feeding of the two owls?
2 Would it be possible for a Barn Owl and a Tawny Owl to live in the same territory? Write down your reasons for giving your answer.

Owl level 10

OWL ARITHMETIC
(You will need a calculator for this task)
(Write your answers on A4 lined paper)

Five pairs of Barn Owls live in one square mile. Between them they capture 24,000 rodents a year.

1 What is a rodent? (use a dictionary if you don't know)
2 How many rodents does ONE of the birds take in a year?
3 How many rodents does ONE bird take in a month?
4 At what time of the year are they likely to take most rodents? Why?
5 Here are some facts about rodents; read them and then try to answer the question:
   - A rodent breeds when it is six months old
   - A pair of rodents produces a litter of young every two months from then on
   - Each litter contains 10 young

   If there are two young rodents on the owl's territory on 1st January 2002, how many do you think there will be on 31st December 2002 if none are killed?
6 If there were no owls, what would happen to the number of rodents on the owl's territory? (Think carefully about the answer.)

EXAMINING THE ROLE OF DIFFERENTIATION THROUGH A CLASSROOM EXAMPLE

So far this chapter has described a teacher's planning, the formulation of learning objectives, and her task-setting strategies, leading to the devising of a series of differentiated tasks for a group of Year 6 students.

We have now looked at some examples of those tasks. This may be an opportune moment to tackle Activity 21.

Activity 21

Critiquing a teacher's differentiation strategies

From the background information given in this chapter, and the task descriptions provided, examine the effectiveness of the teacher's attempt to differentiate work for this class.

Specifically, try to answer the following questions:

- How effective are the plans the teacher has made for dealing with the range of ability within the class?
- What problems do you think the teacher might have encountered in setting up this sequence of differentiated tasks?
- How effective would these tasks have been in providing information about individual students' understanding of the topic?
- From what you can deduce, what additional tasks might the teacher have had to consider, or what other factors might she have had to take into account?
- How important was the element of co-operative work which she introduced into the lesson?
- What would you have done differently?
- Could she have set 'one task for all'? If not, why not?
- As a fellow professional, what elements in this teacher's approach do you particularly warm to or admire?

Tracking, and reporting on, differentiated tasks

Differentiation inevitably means that task-setting becomes a more complicated process. It is for this reason that it is even more important than usual (see Chapter 6) for teachers not only to maintain good records of what tasks are set and to whom, but also to include notes on the outcomes of the learning for individual students and for the class as a whole.

In this section we look briefly at some methods of keeping track of the outcomes of differentiated tasks and obtaining feedback about student learning. Four possible methods are described and evaluated.

1 Small group tutoring

One of the methods now inbuilt into the National Literacy Strategy is for teachers to spend some time with small groups of students performing a common task, while other students are intent on other, individual, tasks. This small group tutoring session is designed so that teachers can gain feedback on the learning of the group, can probe the failures of learning, can probe and extend learning, and can record (make simple notes on) what has been achieved and what still needs to be done. This methodology is useful as far as it goes. Since it is a group activity it may not uncover all the problems of individuals, nor indeed all their achievements. It does depend on a high degree of class control since other students must be gainfully occupied. Time for this activity can be quite limited in most classrooms. Nevertheless, as one strategy among many, it should be in the teacher's armoury.

2 Individual tutoring

This is designed so that a teacher can gain a quite detailed insight into how students are progressing. Many schools now timetable some time into the school term so that teachers can spend short sessions with individuals to check on, and guide, progress. The idea is very sound: in the best of all worlds, perhaps it should be a common occurrence. Many teachers would claim that individual tutoring happens, but they probably think of it as an in-class phenomenon taking only a few seconds. The more sustained conversation of 10 to 30 minutes is, however, a more demanding affair for both parties. The real problem here is time, unless it is programmed into the timetable. If it does take place, there should be some systematic, shared log of the outcomes.

3 Maintaining a learning log

A useful and increasingly widespread ploy is for students to be asked to maintain a learning log – that is, to record in some kind of diary a reflective account of how their learning is progressing. This method utilises the principle of metacognition. It has plenty of value – once students have been trained in the process, and the habit, by the teacher. The big advantage is that the student does the recording, and the teacher has a tangible record which can be taken away and perused at any convenient time, used at Open Evening and so on. It has a built-in flexibility which does not apply to the previous two strategies, but time still needs to be put aside for it.

4 Peer appraisal

An alternative strategy is for students' work to be subject to scrutiny by their peers. In an earlier chapter (Chapter 7) I described the compilation of a Greek newspaper by a primary class. The arbiters of 'quality' in this instance were the 'editors' – three students appointed to that role. They decided whether writing or pictures were 'good enough' to be included. This method is not a substitute for teacher appraisal and recording. It does reflect the reality of life, however: in the world outside school it is peer appraisal that often counts. The danger might lie in whether the students are mature enough to make judgements, and in sensitive individuals feeling threatened by the process. It represents a useful, occasional, device for monitoring outcomes from tasks, but not one to be adopted lightly or for prolonged periods.

Activity 22

Considering monitoring and recording methods for differentiated tasks

Look back over the four methods described in this section for monitoring and recording the outcomes of differentiated tasks. How well would each work in your own situation?

Have you tried each one? If there is any you have not tried, find an opportunity to put it to the test and evaluate it for yourself.

What other methods do you/could you use? What are the comparative strengths and weakness of these?

So, let us try to draw together some of the thoughts about tracking and recording progress of students through differentiated tasks. A range of strategies is open to teachers; but the use and frequency of those strategies must be monitored to ensure an appropriate balance. Strategies are likely to be effective when they increase teacher–student interaction. An eye must be kept on ensuring that, whatever strategies are used, they do not end up by diminishing teaching time significantly.

Assessment and appraisal are a part of the learning process – if well used, a very significant part – by they are not a substitute for other approaches to learning and teaching. While monitoring is in progress for some students, others must be gainfully employed. Where students are given increased freedom to control their own learning (e.g. through the maintenance of learning logs) there must not be loopholes which allow them opportunities for work avoidance or slowing their own progress. The balance of work for all students between whole class, group work and individualised modes must be properly maintained. The use of para-professionals to carry out some support tasks in relation to this monitoring process may need to be considered.

Finally, some thought needs to be given to devising some form of written record for a series of differentiated tasks like the one on Living Things described earlier in this chapter. This, then, becomes your last Activity.

Activity 23

Devising written recording procedures for a differentiated task

Look back over the sequence of 'Owl' related tasks described in this chapter. Devise a written record for this. Your record must include:

- a way of indicating what the tasks are / your learning intentions for them;
- a way of identifying their demand or cognitive level;
- a note of who did which task(s);
- a means for describing achievement in relation to each task;
- a means for identifying future targets for each student/group.

Outcomes

At the end of this chapter you should have:

- Followed the course of an actual series of lessons that comply with both the National Standards, and also with the advice given about formulating learning objectives and setting classroom tasks throughout this book
- Reflected critically on the place and methods of differentiation within the process of teaching and task-setting
- Compared and contrasted the approaches outlined here with your own
- Experimented with methods of monitoring and recording the outcomes of differentiated work by pupils.

11 CONCLUSION: A RATIONALE FOR CLASSROOM LEARNING

The TTA documents (2001, 2002) to which we have referred throughout this book lay down the parameters of successful teaching as it has been recently defined by the Government. These include:

- Subject knowledge;
- Knowledge of the national strategies, e.g. in numeracy and literacy;
- For Key Stage 2, understanding what is expected of teachers in the non-core foundation subjects and RE;
- Understanding of the high standards expected of pupils nationally and locally;
- Knowledge of the principles and practice of entitlement and inclusion for pupils;
- Planning and teaching to clear objectives and setting pupil targets (exactly the ground covered in this book);
- The core pedagogical skills of interactive teaching, differentiation and assessment (covered in a companion volume and in this text);
- Knowledge of behaviour management (covered in John Bryson's manual in this series);
- Understanding how to support pupils with special needs and bilingual pupils.

Teaching is not just about knowing things, and not even about carrying out specific behaviours in an appropriate sequence. The person who is good at a subject but can't communicate his or her knowledge is not a teacher, because communication is at the heart of teaching. Teaching that is predicated on the view that teachers can just reproduce behaviours (the competency approach) and all will be well in the classroom, reduces the teacher at best to a technician and at worst to an automaton. In real classrooms, which are peopled by many and highly individual youngsters, these behaviours simply don't work. By contrast, we often hear about 'teaching style' – an elusive concept to define and illustrate – but one which holds an important key. The key is this: it is not the package of skills alone that is important in effective teaching, it is the way those skills are used with judgement and in the context of the personality of the teacher and taught that defines this style. Legislating for teacher competence is nigh on impossible; but defining the mix of skills, qualities and behaviours that go to make up a successful practitioner is a better starting point. In this book, an attempt has been made to take three areas of teaching skills, to rehearse the skills needed in each area, and to place those skills in a context of professionalism that might begin to define their effectiveness.

In the earlier TTA document (2001) this process is described under the title 'Professional Values and Practice'. These consist of teachers:

- Having high expectations of pupils, valuing and respecting their diverse cultural, religious and ethnic backgrounds, and being committed to raising educational achievement (para 1.1);
- Treating pupils with respect, consistency and consideration – and as individuals – with a view to developing their abilities (para 1.2);
- Acting as role models to demonstrate the positive values, attitudes and behaviour that are expected of the students (para 1.3);
- Having the ability to communicate with relevant adults in and outside the school (para 1.4) including those in support and other professional roles (para 1.6).

There are broader aspects to this professionalism, too, in the view of the TTA document (2001) and they are relevant to this book. In addition to contributing to the overall life of the school and its extra-curricular activities (para 1.5), and understanding the legal frameworks within which teachers work (para 1.9), teachers have to take responsibility for their own development as professionals.

This text is one way of doing that. The TTA requires that teachers:

- Have the motivation and ability to take increasing responsibility for their own professional development (para 1.7), and
- Are able to improve their own teaching by evaluating it, by learning from the effective practice of others and by using research, inspection and other evidence (para 1.8).

These are precisely the intentions of this book (and of this whole series). But it is worth pausing over this point. The trend in thinking about teaching over the last two decades has been increasingly to identify the need for continuing professional development. That is logical enough in an era of rapid change, as we identified in the Editorial. But being briefed about new developments is not enough. Many of these developments have an effect on practice: on how material is presented, on how it is assessed, evaluated, recorded and so on. Alongside the opportunities for development, theories of development have evolved. We expect teachers to be reflective practitioners: to look objectively at practice (including their own) and to learn from it. But we also expect them to experiment: in effect, to become their own researchers. The tenets of action research have never been more significant.

Action research may sound an esoteric process, but at root it is really very simple. It suggests that the teacher identifies a classroom problem, hypothesises a way of dealing with it more effectively, puts the proposed solution into practice, notes the results from this action, evaluates their effectiveness, and then either modifies their own behaviour or manipulates the solution in order to achieve a more effective lesson.

In the present case, for example, one might imagine a case where a young teacher adopts a record-keeping system for pupils' work, but then finds at parents' evening that this simply doesn't help her conversations with the parents (the problem). She analyses the difficulties the recording system has caused her, and remodels her system to a new experimental one (the hypothesis). For the next term she keep records in the new format. At the next parents' evening she uses this new format (the experiment) and makes notes of how well it works or fails to work (the evidence). She then makes some minor modifications to the system (modifies the solution) but adopts this new modified procedure (i.e. she modifies her own behaviour). She has been engaged, consciously or not, in action research.

This reflective approach (researching one's own behaviour), and reflexive action (changing one's behaviour in line with the outcomes of one's researches), is now a cornerstone of teaching. Initiatives such as the Government's Best Practice scholarships to enable teachers to research in their own institutions under guidance from skilled external researchers is a signal that this approach is currently in favour. The intended outcome from such an approach is probably well summarised by Hay McBer (*Introduction*):

> *Effective teachers in the future will need to deal with a climate of continual change in which distance learning and other teaching media will become more prevalent. The 'star teachers' of the future will be those who work to make what is now the best become the standard for all.*

But, whatever is said in legislation or guidance, maintaining professionalism is essentially a personal thing. It is about accountability, but above all about accountability to oneself. To end this book I would like to illustrate what I am saying with the following short story.

An old saddle-maker took on an apprentice. The boy was good at his job and learned well. His skills were potentially beyond those of his master. The boy served out his apprenticeship, and the time was coming for him to make his final test-piece before setting up as a craftsman in his own right. The old man watched him work, with great pride, for he had taught him all he knew. But as he watched, the boy drove one nail home just short of true. It was on the underside of the saddle and would be covered by a fold of leather in the finished work. As the boy worked, the old man put his hand on his arm. 'Why didn't you draw that nail and replace it?' he asked. 'No one will see it,' replied the boy. 'No, but one person will always know the work is less than perfect,' said the old man, 'and will you be satisfied with that?'

As professionals we should believe in accountability, but as part of our personal integrity.

So we set the learning objectives of our lessons because that is how learning can best operate. Once set, we have to try to deliver the lessons we want to be learned using our armoury of skills. In a companion book in the series we have looked at learning achieved through insightful questioning and through effective explaining. In this book the emphasis has been on setting tasks that make demands on students' cognitive processes. Whatever method we choose for the lesson – these or others – it has to be handled with skill. This book has suggested that the best tasks have to be planned to meet the needs and match the abilities of the learners, and it has offered some insights into the skills of setting tasks.

In turn, the processes of meeting and matching mean that one task is often unlikely to be suitable for every student. The 'one size fits all' of the retail trade is hardly a professional slogan for developing young minds. So differentiation is needed to try to match tasks more effectively to need. It is a subtle business, as teachers have identified in the research which was reported in Chapters 8 and 9.

In the twenty-first century there can be little doubt that public and political involvement in schools will increase rather than diminish. This is not a bad thing, though it sometimes is thought to be so. But it does turn the spotlight on any inadequacies in teaching and learning. For the professionals that means that they have to be increasingly sure of their skills, able to articulate why they act as they do, and secure in taking control of their own profession and of their own professional development. It is as a contribution to this process that this teaching skills' series is offered.

LIST OF ACTIVITIES

LIST OF FIGURES

LIST OF TABLES

INDEX